MW00772784

PRAISE FOR *THROUGH THE YEAR WITH JESUS*

"Katherine Bogner hits a liturgical living home run with this devotional for children. The readings and reflections are weighty and meaningful, yet simple to do and understand. The Lectio Divina method of encountering Scripture is ancient and profound, yet relevant and doable for modern families. We get great works of art, plus the tools to appreciate and interpret them. This book is an excellent, all-in-one way to bring the stories of Jesus and His family and His friends and His life into a home or classroom in a way that kids of all ages can connect with at their own levels. Grownups are sure to find their own faith deepened as well."

Kendra Tierney, Author of *The Catholic All Year Compendium*

"The content is rich and helpful. The layout is incredibly user-friendly. The writing is approachable yet thoughtful. If you've been looking for a way to engage your family or classroom in meaningful conversations throughout the liturgical year here is your answer. Buy this book!"

Bonnie Engstrom, Author of *61 Minutes to a Miracle*

"This book is a treasure. *Through the Year with Jesus* not only has beautiful Scripture readings and reflections on the Gospels, it is also an invaluable guide to help parents, teachers, and catechists learn *how* to pray through the Bible with their children—and how to teach *them* to pray and live God's Word. This will be a frequently used and well-loved resource in our home!"

Katie Warner, Catholic Children's Book Author, FirstFaithTreasury.com

"Lectio Divina (and Visio Divina) are the hidden gems of prayer in the Catholic Church. With this book, Katherine Bogner brings these devotions to life for children, teachers, and parents. I am certain her guidance here will lead many young people into an encounter with Jesus Christ. This is a great resource for classrooms and homes."

Jared Dees, Founder of TheReligionTeacher.com and Author of *Christ in the Classroom*

"*Through the Year with Jesus* is a powerful resource capable of inviting children to authentically engage with their Savior, Jesus Christ. Bogner understands how children's hearts grow closer to Christ: in the silence, through stories, and through action. *Through the Year with Jesus* offers children and adults alike a beautiful plan for walking through the year with Jesus."

Nancy Bandzuch, Founder and Creative Director of Catholic Sprouts

"Nurturing holy families takes work and a healthy assist. *Through the Year with Jesus* is one such resource. You certainly could read it in one sitting, but I love that it's the kind of book that breathes with life. A family can pick it up as the liturgical season progresses, diving deep in Scripture, memorizing Bible verses, seeing the parallels between the Word and our daily lives, or simply doing *Visio Divina*. It meets families right where they are, in all our imperfections, and gives us the tools to wrap our children in God's word. What a blessing to so many families!"

Kathryn Whitaker, Author of *Live Big, Love Bigger*

"What a tremendous gift to the Church this book is! Parents, grandparents, godparents, teachers, and friends will find the Gospels opened to them through these reflections, questions, and (most especially) the insights they glean from the children they love. *Through the Year with Jesus* is an invaluable resource for any family or classroom, for anyone who wants to know Jesus better through Scripture."

Meg Hunter-Kilmer, Speaker and Author of *Saints Around the World*

"We're told as parents that we're the primary educators of our children, but often that can feel more daunting than empowering! In *Through the Year With Jesus*, Katherine Bogner gives parents the tools we need to share the faith as a family and to grow in faith and prayer alongside our children. Children (and parents!) of all ages are sure to deepen their faith with the practical guidance in this treasure of a book!"

Rosie Hill, Homeschooling Mom of 7 and Catholic Blogger

"As the Superintendent of Schools for the Catholic Diocese of Peoria, what a delight it has been to observe and benefit from the many, many gifts of teaching and creativity that Katherine continues to share in our schools. As

I read *Through the Year With Jesus* I was overwhelmed with emotion as I thought of how God has used this beautiful and talented young woman to share the love that she has for His Son in a way that allows us to encounter Him each and every day. Thank you, Katherine!"

Dr. Sharon Weiss, Superintendent of Schools, Catholic Diocese of Peoria, Illinois

"In Matthew 19:14, Jesus says, 'Let the children come to me, and do not hinder them; for to such belongs the kingdom of heaven.' If you want to know as a family or as an individual how to fulfill the mandate of letting children come to Jesus and to know, serve, and love Him, this book is a definitive resource. Katherine Bogner does not only love children and teaching them; she is exemplary and committed in her faith as a Catholic."

Rev. Fr. John Bosco Mujuni, Ed.D, Pastor, Immaculate Conception Parish, Lacon, Illinois

"Long have I searched for a book that makes Scripture accessible to every child and family. This book helps you not only to know about Jesus but to know Him through a personal relationship with Him in prayer. It is a cornerstone book for every child, family, church, school, teacher, and catechist."

Jenny Witt, Director of Evangelization, St. Philomena Catholic Church, Peoria, Illinois

THROUGH THE *year*

WITH *Jesus*

GOSPEL READINGS AND
REFLECTIONS FOR CHILDREN

THROUGH THE Year WITH Jesus

GOSPEL READINGS AND
REFLECTIONS FOR CHILDREN

KATHERINE BOGNER

EMMAUS
ROAD
PUBLISHING

Emmaus Road Publishing
1468 Parkview Circle
Steubenville, Ohio 43952

Library of Congress Control Number: 2020952014
978-1-64585-084-7 hardcover | 978-1-64585-086-1 ebook

Cover design and layout by Patty Borgman
Nihil obstat:
Msgr. Philip D. Halfacre, V.G.
Censor Librorum

Imprimatur:
Most Rev. Daniel R. Jenky, C.S.C.
Bishop of Peoria

23 October 2020

DEDICATION

Dedicated to the Holy Family,
whose Sacred Heart, Immaculate Heart, and Pure Heart
have taught me how to love.

And to my own holy family who loves me so well.
Dad, Steph, Steven, Violet, Oliver, Evan, Emily, Luke, Theodore, & Declan

In loving memory of
Rebecca Sue Bogner

TABLE OF CONTENTS

The Life of Jesus & the Liturgical Year   xiii

A Note for Parents and Teachers   xv

A Guide to Lectio Divina with Children   xvii

A Note on Visio Divina   xix

A Guide to the Rosary   xx

THE SEASON OF ADVENT   1

Visio Divina for Advent: *The Annunciation*, Bl. Fra Angelico   2

The Annunciation: 1st Week of Advent   3

The Visitation: 2nd Week of Advent   6

Joseph's Dream: 3rd Week of Advent   9

The Nativity: 4th Week of Advent   12

THE SEASON OF CHRISTMAS   15

Visio Divina for Christmas: *The Nativity*, Federico Barocci   16

The Visit of the Shepherds: Feast of the Holy Family   17

The Visit of the Magi: Epiphany   20

THE SEASON OF ORDINARY TIME I   23

Visio Divina for Ordinary Time: *The Baptism of Christ*, Francesco Trevisani   24

The Baptism of Jesus: Baptism of the Lord   25

The Presentation in the Temple: 2nd Week of Ordinary Time   28

The Holy Family in Nazareth: 3rd Week of Ordinary Time   31

The Finding of Jesus in the Temple: 4th Week of Ordinary Time   34

The Word of God: 5th Week of Ordinary Time   37

Visio Divina for Ordinary Time: *The Wedding Feast at Cana*, Tintoretto   40

The Wedding at Cana: 6th Week of Ordinary Time   41

The Call of the Disciples: 7th Week of Ordinary Time   45

THE SEASON OF LENT   48

Visio Divina for Lent: *The Crucifixion*, Diego Velázquez   49

The Temptation in the Desert: 1st Week of Lent   50

The Preaching of John the Baptist: 2nd Week of Lent   54

The Agony in the Garden: 3rd Week of Lent   57

The Scourging at the Pillar: 4th Week of Lent   61

The Crowning with Thorns: 5th Week of Lent   64

The Carrying of the Cross: 6th Week of Lent   67

THE SACRED TRIDUUM   70

Visio Divina for the Triduum: *Jesus Is Placed in the Tomb*, Albin and Paul Windhausen   71

The Last Supper: Holy Thursday   72

The Crucifixion and Death of Jesus: Good Friday   75

The Burial of Jesus: Holy Saturday   79

THE SEASON OF EASTER   82

Visio Divina for Easter: *The Resurrection of Christ*, Paolo Veronese   83

The Resurrection: Easter   84

Jesus Appears to Thomas: Divine Mercy   88

Visio Divina for Easter: *Landscape with Christ and His Disciples on the Road to Emmaus*, Jan Wildens   91

The Road to Emmaus: 3rd Week of Easter   92

The Good Shepherd: 4th Week of Easter   96

Power to Forgive: 5th Week of Easter   99

Jesus and Peter at the Sea of Tiberias: 6th Week of Easter   102

The Ascension: 7th Week of Easter   105

Visio Divina for Easter: *Pentecost*, Jean II Restout   108

The Descent of the Holy Spirit: Pentecost   109

THE SEASON OF ORDINARY TIME II   112

Visio Divina for Ordinary Time: *The Sacred Heart of Jesus*, Artist Unknown   113

The Spirit of Truth: Most Holy Trinity   114

The Bread of Life Discourse: Body and Blood of Christ   117

The Beatitudes: 11th Week of Ordinary Time   120

The Blessing of the Children: 12th Week of Ordinary Time   123

Visio Divina for Ordinary Time: *Let the Little Children Come to Me*, Gebhard Fugel   126

The Lord's Prayer: 13th Week of Ordinary Time   127

Peter's Confession about Jesus: 14th Week of Ordinary Time   130

The Woman at the Well: 15th Week of Ordinary Time   133

Blind Bartimaeus: 16th Week of Ordinary Time   136

The Parable of the Lost Sheep: 17th Week of Ordinary Time   139

The Raising of Lazarus: 18th Week of Ordinary Time   142

The Parable of the Mustard Seed: 19th Week of Ordinary Time   145

Two Miraculous Healings: 20th Week of Ordinary Time   148

Visio Divina for Ordinary Time: *The Sermon on the Mount,* Carl Bloch   151

The Feeding of the Five Thousand: 21st Week of Ordinary Time   152

The Transfiguration: 22nd Week of Ordinary Time   156

Walking on Water: 23rd Week of Ordinary Time   159

The Prodigal Son: 24th Week of Ordinary Time   162

The Healing of a Paralytic: 25th Week of Ordinary Time   166

Ask, Seek, Knock: 26th Week of Ordinary Time   169

The Greatest Commandment: 27th Week of Ordinary Time   172

Visio Divina for Ordinary Time: *Christ's Entry into Jerusalem*,
Jean-Hippolyte Flandrin   175

The Entry into Jerusalem: 28th Week of Ordinary Time   176

The Anointing at Bethany: 29th Week of Ordinary Time   179

The Parable of the Wedding Feast: 30th Week of Ordinary Time   182

Washing the Feet of the Disciples: 31st Week of Ordinary Time   186

The Vine and the Branches: 32nd Week of Ordinary Time   189

The Judgement of the Nations: 33rd Week of Ordinary Time   192

The Coming of the Son of Man: Christ the King   196

Visio Divina for Ordinary Time: *The Disputation of the Blessed Sacrament*,
Raphael   199

Afterword   201

Acknowledgements   202

Attributions   204

THE LIFE OF JESUS & THE LITURGICAL YEAR

We all love listening to stories. The good guys and bad guys, patterns and surprises, struggle and victory—each element of good storytelling can captivate us no matter our age. Stories model life around us, teach and form us, and are the tool with which we share ourselves with others.

God, who is outside of time, knows how narrative shapes our days. Our own ability to tell stories elevates us above all of creation and shows that we were made in the image and likeness of the Creator. So it shouldn't surprise us that the Bible is the most wonderful story ever told, most especially because it is so much more than a story—it is all true, and it all leads to everlasting life.

We learn about Jesus, the Second Person of the Trinity, through stories. The events of Jesus' life have characters and setting, conflicts and resolutions, as well as morals and lessons. But beyond words on a page, we are invited to enter into a story which is living and active. Intended for each person in every era, we walk through the life of Christ not only in the Bible but also in the way we celebrate the liturgical year. From the readings we hear at Mass, the pattern of feasting and fasting, and the traditions that we keep in remembrance, the rhythm of our worship is wrapped around the events of Jesus' time on earth.

I often joke with my students that the Church is awfully wise in the way we celebrate the liturgical year. Imagine if we walked through the events in Jesus' life, but in real time. So after hearing the story of the Annunciation, we would wait nine months for Christmas. Following that, it would be twelve years until the Finding in the Temple . . . and then another eighteen years until Jesus' Baptism! All in all, it would be thirty-three years between Christmases (and this is when my students gasp and groan). Instead of waiting so long to learn and celebrate and pray with these Mysteries, the Church in her wisdom helps us grow in faith with these events in and out of each and every year.

We gather around the manger with Mary and Joseph. We stand in awe as Jesus is baptized in the Jordan River and begins His public ministry. We hear Him call His disciples and follow along for three years of miracles and teachings. We watch day by day during His Passion, Death, and Resurrection. Year after year, as they are repeated, these stories form a spiral that deepens our understanding and draws us nearer and nearer to the heart of Christ.

The liturgical year is an invitation to walk with Christ in an incarnational and tangible way. This book is a tool for facilitating that encounter in homes and classrooms, revealing the rich mystery of the seasons as we celebrate. Each entry is intended to start conversations throughout the week with children and help make the stories of Jesus come alive.

It is my deepest hope and prayer that this book points you and the children in your life to a new understanding of the Bible. It is the greatest story ever told and has the power to lead us to a deep and abiding love for Christ and His Church.

A NOTE FOR PARENTS AND TEACHERS

The intention of this book is to invite you and your children or students to more deeply encounter Christ through the rhythm of the liturgical year and the beauty of Scripture. For each week of the year, a short passage from the Gospels has been chosen for you to read, pray with, and discuss.

The table of contents shares suggested readings according to the week of the liturgical calendar, which changes slightly each year. Because the Sunday Mass readings follow a three-year cycle, this book instead offers an overview of Christ's ministry and mission inspired by the pattern of the liturgical year.

The two chunks of Ordinary Time vary in length, so you might have to jump around in this book based on how the seasons fall. To accommodate for other variations, there are a few extra Sundays included in the book to ensure you have a relevant reading for each week. Stories that could be used as meditations while praying the Mysteries of the Rosary are also marked on page xx.

No matter what order you read the stories in, these Gospel passages can help form a well-rounded understanding of the Life of Christ, from the Annunciation and Nativity, to His teaching and ministry, to His Passion, Death, and Resurrection.

The content included to support reading each Scripture passage can be used for one long lesson or broken up in pieces over the week. Feel free to choose the sections that work best for your home or classroom and adapt according to the age and interest of the children. Find times that work best in your routine to encourage discussion and prayer, continuing the conversation past a single reading of the story. Time in the car, gathering together for meals, downtime after playing outside, or right before bed are all opportunities to bring your faith into practice. Here are a few ideas for the content included each week:

◆ MEMORY VERSE: For each week, a short verse is included to help reinforce the message of the Gospel. Use it as an aid to prayer or for Scripture memorization. Feel free to memorize the verse provided or choose a different one while you read.

◆ READ GOD'S WORD: This section recommends a story about Jesus to read and one place to find it. The text from the Scriptures (Revised Standard Version, 2nd Catholic Edition) is included. Remember, many of these stories can be found in more than one Gospel, so you can even compare and contrast. Don't be afraid to read the story straight from your Bible, but feel free to look at it in short sections depending on the age of your children.

You also can use a favorite Children's Bible or adapted version that better suits your needs. And don't forget that the Bible is available online and through many apps, so you also can read or listen on the go!

◆ **TELL THE STORY:** Here you are provided with a child-friendly reflection on the story. Use this in your own words to help make the Gospel passage more relatable and relevant. This section includes a set of conversation starters. These questions are intended to continue the conversation after you read the weekly Scripture selection. Each is perfect to pose over a meal or while going for a walk to keep everyone thinking about the message God has for them. This is a great section to help stretch the content between younger and older kids by varying the questions and connections.

◆ **LIVE IT OUT:** In this section, a simple idea is shared for bringing the story into family or classroom life. It might include further background on the passage, an idea for an activity, a prayer to share together, a virtue to pursue, or wisdom from a saint. While this is meant to be an inspiration to support liturgical living, you also can also dig into the wealth of resources online to find great recipes, crafts, and activities to go along with the story of the week. (Some suggestions are CatholicAllYear.com, CatholicIcing.com, Lazy Liturgical resources from CallHerHappy.com, and all the free resources on my blog, LookToHimAndBeRadiant.com.)

◆ **LECTIO DIVINA:** A special section includes prompts for praying with the Scripture passage using Lectio Divina, which can help you turn reading Scripture into a prayer. Check out the next page for more ideas for using Lectio Divina with kids.

Note that you can use any of these steps for as little (or as much) time as you want. It can be done quietly, with discussion, or through journaling.

A GUIDE TO LECTIO DIVINA WITH CHILDREN

Reading the Bible doesn't have to be intimidating. Lectio Divina is an ancient prayer practice that can make Scripture come alive. It is a useful tool for all ages, whether you are four years old or one-hundred-and-four years old.

Lectio Divina, meaning "Divine Reading" in Latin, can act as a guide to help you dive into stories from the Bible to encounter God and the message He has for each of you. Lectio Divina works best with short passages (even just one verse) prayed with over a period of time.

A simplified version of the steps is *Read, Think, Pray, and Listen.* First we read the story, then we think about what it is saying. Next, we pray and listen for God's response. The whole process can be done in less than five minutes when kids are young or just learning how to do Lectio Divina on their own.

Below are some details for the four traditional steps in Lectio Divina and ideas on how you might use this method to pray with a story or passage from the Bible. Depending on age-appropriateness, you can use the steps and reflection questions to think aloud as a family or class, to give inspiration for a time of quiet prayer, or even to guide prayer journaling. Specific reflections for each step are also provided with each weekly Scripture selection.

LECTIO = READ
+ Read the selected section several times, be attentive to detail
+ Note verses or phrases that stand out to you, work to understand meaning and background
+ Prayer starter:
    • In this passage . . .
    • My favorite verse was . . .
    • I noticed . . .

MEDITATIO = MEDITATE
+ Think about the reading and connect it to your life
+ Imagine being present to hear the passage or witness the story
+ Prayer starter:
    • This reminds me of . . .
    • If I were there . . .
    • I can connect this story to . . .

ORATIO = PRAY
+ Dialogue with God in prayer about the passage
+ Thank God for His Word

- Ask Him to lead you into deeper understanding
- Prayer starter:
  - Dear Jesus . . .
  - Thank you God for . . .
  - Please help me understand . . .

CONTEMPLATIO = CONTEMPLATE

- Quiet expression of love between you and God
- Take time to listen
- Note what God is trying to teach you through the passage and time of prayer
- Prayer starter:
  - I think Jesus is teaching me . . .
  - Lord, I love you for . . .
  - I believe . . .

A NOTE ON VISIO DIVINA

Children and adults alike learn more using visual components. Visio Divina ("Divine Seeing") follows the same steps as Lectio Divina but draws from Sacred Art rather than Sacred Scripture. This book provides many classic paintings to study throughout the Liturgical Seasons, but you can always search for meaningful art online to match the story of the week and then use the same process for a corresponding painting. The rich details and artist's interpretation can help us explore the Gospel through a new lens and aid children in forming a mental image of their own for the event in Jesus' life.

Pull up the artwork on a big screen or project it onto the wall so that children can see all the details clearly. Allow them to spend a few minutes silently looking at the image before discussing. The prompts provided can guide discussion or be used for journaling.

A GUIDE TO THE ROSARY

The beauty of the Rosary is that it is not just a method of meditative prayer; it is also essentially a Bible study on a string. Using the Mysteries of the Rosary, we walk through highlighted events in Christ's life and are given time to dwell on the meaning of each story.

When praying the Rosary with kids, less can be more. Instead of always focusing on praying through five decades at a time, sometimes it is nice to slow down and zoom in on one particular Mystery.

Using the reflections in this book, introduce and discuss the story as found in the Gospels before or during the prayers of the decade. The twenty Mysteries of the Rosary and their locations in the book are organized here for your convenience.

"The rosary is the book of the blind, where souls see and there enact the greatest drama of love the world has ever known; it is the book of the simple, which initiates them into mysteries and knowledge more satisfying than the education of other men; it is the book of the aged, whose eyes close upon the shadow of this world, and open on the substance of the next. The power of the rosary is beyond description."

— *Archbishop Fulton J. Sheen* —

JOYFUL MYSTERIES
Pray on Monday and Saturday

- The Annunciation, page 3
- The Visitation, page 6
- The Nativity, page 12
- The Presentation in the Temple, page 28
- The Finding of Jesus in the Temple, page 34

SORROWFUL MYSTERIES
Pray on Tuesday and Friday

- The Agony in the Garden, page 57

- The Scourging at the Pillar, page 61
- The Crowning with Thorns, page 64
- The Carrying of the Cross, page 67
- The Crucifixion and Death of Jesus, page 75

GLORIOUS MYSTERIES
Pray on Wednesday and Sunday
- The Resurrection, page 84
- The Ascension, page 105
- The Descent of the Holy Spirit, page 109
- The Assumption of Mary *(See 1 Cor 15:20–27; suggested reading: Holy Family in Nazareth)*, page 31
- The Coronation of Mary *(See Rev 12:1–5; suggested reading: The Judgement of the Nations)*, page 192

LUMINOUS MYSTERIES
Pray on Thursday
- The Baptism of Jesus, page 25
- The Wedding at Cana, page 41
- The Proclamation of the Gospel *(The Beatitudes)*, page 120
- The Transfiguration, page 156
- The Institution of the Eucharist *(The Last Supper)*, page 72

THE SEASON OF Advent

Advent is a season of waiting.

We wait for this year's celebration of Christmas, preparing our hearts to be ready to celebrate the birth of the Newborn King.

During Advent we also remember the waiting of the Israelites over many centuries for the coming Messiah. The whole Old Testament records the story of God's people looking with hope toward the time when God would send the promised Savior. We also wait with Mary and Joseph for Jesus to be born, reading the stories of their experiences from the Annunciation to the Nativity.

What are you waiting on in your life? Advent is a time to grow in virtue and ultimately trust in God while you wait.

Advent is also a season of wonder.

We feel awe and amazement that the almighty and powerful God would become man in the form of a tiny baby in the Blessed Virgin Mary's womb.

Wonder and awe, also called Fear of the Lord, is a Gift of the Holy Spirit. Fear of the Lord does not mean that we are afraid. It is a gift that reminds us that while we are small and finite, God is all-powerful and infinite.

Advent is an awe-inspiring time of year when we are given the opportunity to reflect on the great gift of Jesus' Incarnation. The wonder we feel as we contemplate the work of God should fill our hearts, helping us to wait with hope.

Advent teaches us that God's wonderful plan is always worth waiting for.

"When you became small, O God, you made human beings great."

ST. CATHERINE OF SIENA

VISIO DIVINA FOR ADVENT
The Annunciation *by Bl. Fra Angelico*

The Annunciation, *Fra Angelico, 1430*

Try Visio Divina with this painting of St. Gabriel's Annunciation to Mary by Bl. Fra Angelico. Use the same steps as in Lectio Divina: Lectio, Meditatio, Oratio, Contemplatio.

First, slowly examine the art, noticing details and how it tells a story. Then, think about the painting and make connections to what you already know. Finally, take a few minutes to pray about the image, asking God questions as well as listening to what He shares with you.

REFLECTION QUESTIONS

◆ Identify all the characters in the painting. Can you find Mary, Gabriel, Adam, and Eve?
◆ Where is the light coming from in the picture?
◆ What emotions do you see in each person's expression?

THE ANNUNCIATION

The 1st Week of Advent

LUKE 1:26–38

In the sixth month the angel Gabriel was sent from God to a city of Galilee named Nazareth, to a virgin betrothed to a man whose name was Joseph, of the house of David; and the virgin's name was Mary. And he came to her and said, "Hail, full of grace, the Lord is with you!" But she was greatly troubled at the saying, and considered in her mind what sort of greeting this might be.

"Behold, I am the handmaid of the Lord; let it be to me according to your word."

— Luke 1:38 —

And the angel said to her, "Do not be afraid, Mary, for you have found favor with God. And behold, you will conceive in your womb and bear a son, and you shall call his name him Jesus. He will be great, and will be called the Son of the Most High; and the Lord God will give to him the throne of his father David, and he will reign over the house of Jacob for ever; and of his kingdom there will be no end."

And Mary said to the angel, "How can this be, since I have no husband?" And the angel said to her, "The Holy Spirit will come upon you, and the power of the Most High will overshadow you; therefore the child to be born will be called holy, the Son of God. And behold, your kinswoman Elizabeth in her old age has also conceived a son; and this is the sixth month with her who was called barren. For with God nothing will be impossible."

And Mary said, "Behold, I am the handmaid of the Lord; let it be to me according to your word." And the angel departed from her.

TELL THE *Story*

When you ask your mom and dad a question, sometimes they say "Yes," sometimes they say "No," and sometimes they say "Not right now." Thousands of years before this story happened, God had asked the first man and woman a question, and they had answered "no" with their choices.

Adam and Eve hadn't trusted God, but He still loved them and promised a Messiah would come to save them. God's people had to wait . . . and wait . . . and wait. But in the fullness of time, God again asked another question, this time to Mary of Nazareth. And she said yes!

Mary trusted God with her whole heart and wanted to do His will. At the Annunciation, God became man as a tiny baby in Mary's womb. During Advent, we wait with hope for that baby to be born!

- Pretend you were peeking through Mary's window at the Annunciation. How would you describe what happened?
- Mary was able to respond to St. Gabriel's message without fear. Why do you think Mary could say yes to God without being afraid?
- After saying yes, she had to wait nine months for Jesus to be born. Inspired by Mary, what can we do together to get ready while we wait for Jesus' birth this Christmas?

Live IT OUT

During Advent, set aside a little time for quiet in your day. Decide when that silence will be and how you will use it. Even five minutes can be a start to developing a habit of quiet prayer, so don't be afraid to start small. Prayerfulness can help us to be like Mary, with a heart open to what God asks of us. Through time in prayer, we can be ready to listen to the amazing plans God has in store for our lives.

LECTIO DIVINA

LECTIO
What did the angel tell Mary? And how did Mary respond?

MEDITATIO
What questions would you like to ask the Archangel Gabriel?

ORATIO
Ask Jesus to help you welcome Him into your heart like Mary did.

CONTEMPLATIO
Think about the nine months that Mary carried Jesus in her womb.

THE VISITATION

The 2nd Week of Advent

LUKE 1:39–56

In those days Mary arose and went with haste into the hill country, to a city of Judah, and she entered the house of Zechariah and greeted Elizabeth.

And when Elizabeth heard the greeting of Mary, the child leaped in her womb; and Elizabeth was filled with the Holy Spirit and she exclaimed with a loud cry, "Blessed are you among women, and blessed is the fruit of your womb! And why is this granted me, that the mother of my Lord should come to me? For behold, when the voice of your greeting came to my ears, the child in my womb leaped for joy. And blessed is she who believed that there would be a fulfilment of what was spoken to her from the Lord."

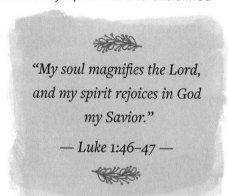

"My soul magnifies the Lord, and my spirit rejoices in God my Savior."

— Luke 1:46-47 —

And Mary said,
"My soul magnifies the Lord,
and my spirit rejoices in God my Savior,
for he has regarded the low estate of his handmaiden.
For behold, henceforth all generations will call me blessed;
for he who is mighty has done great things for me,
and holy is his name.
And his mercy is on those who fear him
from generation to generation.
He has shown strength with his arm,
he has scattered the proud in the imagination of their hearts,
he has put down the mighty from their thrones,
and exalted those of low degree;
he has filled the hungry with good things,
and the rich he has sent empty away.
He has helped his servant Israel,
in remembrance of his mercy,
as he spoke to our fathers,
to Abraham and to his posterity for ever."

And Mary remained with her about three months, and returned to her home.

LECTIO DIVINA

LECTIO
What are some ways Mary describes God in her Magnificat?

MEDITATIO
Imagine seeing Mary and Elizabeth's greeting. What would their time together have been like?

ORATIO
Ask Jesus to help you notice people in need and be quick to help them.

CONTEMPLATIO
Think about how John the Baptist recognized Jesus when he was still in Elizabeth's womb. Ponder how you can be ready to recognize Jesus in your life.

TELL THE *Story*

Have you ever gone a long time between seeing someone you love? Or have you ever had super exciting news to share?

The Blessed Virgin Mary must have felt that kind of eager expectation as she traveled to see her relative Elizabeth. After receiving the message of the angel Gabriel and saying yes to becoming the Mother of God, Mary couldn't wait to talk to Elizabeth, who was expecting a miraculous baby of her own. The two families must have been a great comfort to one another while they awaited the birth of John the Baptist and Jesus!

◆ What do you think Mary's journey was like? What was she thinking about as she got closer to Elizabeth and Zechariah's house?
◆ Mary went to help her relative Elizabeth as she waited for John the Baptist to be born. What are some ways our family helps other people? How has our family received help?
◆ Mary and Elizabeth shared a deep trust in God, and they must have talked about the plan God had in store while they were together. When she arrived, Mary prayed the Magnificat, which is a beautiful song of praise. What are some of your favorite ways to praise God?

Live IT OUT

This week, in honor of the Visitation, make a plan to visit someone and lend a helping hand. Think of a person in your family, a friend, or someone at your parish who maybe has a new baby, is recovering from an illness or surgery, or could use some special visitors. Stop by with a simple meal and some handmade cards.

Advent is a great time to both pray for those in need as well as offer them practical help, just like Mary offered Elizabeth.

JOSEPH'S DREAM
The 3rd Week of Advent

MATTHEW 1:18–25

Now the birth of Jesus Christ took place in this way. When his mother Mary had been betrothed to Joseph, before they came together she was found to be with child of the Holy Spirit; and her husband Joseph, being a just man and unwilling to put her to shame, resolved to send her away quietly.

"When Joseph woke from sleep, he did as the angel of the Lord commanded him."

— Matthew 1:24 —

But as he considered this, behold, an angel of the Lord appeared to him in a dream, saying, "Joseph, son of David, do not fear to take Mary your wife, for that which is conceived in her is of the Holy Spirit; she will bear a son, and you shall call his name Jesus, for he will save his people from their sins."

All this took place to fulfil what the Lord had spoken by the prophet:

"Behold, a virgin shall conceive and bear a son, and his name shall be called Emmanuel"

(which means, God with us). When Joseph woke from sleep, he did as the angel of the Lord commanded him; he took his wife, but knew her not until she had borne a son; and he called his name Jesus.

TELL THE *Story*

Just as God chose Mary out of all women to be the mother of Jesus, He also chose Joseph to be the guardian of the Holy Family.

St. Joseph was a carpenter by trade, and the Bible tells us he was a righteous and holy man. He was both a man of prayer and of action, which was exactly the combination Jesus and Mary needed. In this story, we hear about one of the miraculous dreams Joseph experienced as God guided him in his role. Another of his dreams led the Holy Family to safety in Egypt after Jesus was born. While it might seem crazy to listen to instructions from a dream, Joseph was already pursuing the will of God. It is always easier to be obedient when you are already moving in the right direction, and St. Joseph shows us that God can help us accomplish amazing things if we are ready to listen and willing to act.

- There are no recorded words of St. Joseph in the Bible. Why do you think the Holy Spirit chose to show him as a man of action rather than of words?
- What do you think went through Joseph's mind when he first woke up from his dream?
- What are some ways you can act on the things God asks of you?

IT OUT

The themes of the four weeks of Advent are hope, peace, joy, and love.

We often count down and remember the virtue of the week using an Advent wreath with three purple candles and one rose candle. The rose candle is for the third week and represents the joy that the birth of Jesus is drawing near. Your church probably has an Advent wreath on display during this season, but you can make one for your family as well!

The home of the Holy Family must have overflowed with hope, peace, joy, and love. Make a list of ways you see each of these gifts in your family, home, friends, school, church, and community. How can you grow in hope, peace, joy, and love between now and Christmas?

LECTIO DIVINA

LECTIO
What message did the angel give St. Joseph?

MEDITATIO
How did Joseph respond? What would you have done?

ORATIO
Ask your Guardian Angel to help you be attentive to the messages of God.

CONTEMPLATIO
Close your eyes and imagine what Joseph's dream must have been like.

THE NATIVITY

The 4th Week of Advent

LUKE 2:1–14

In those days a decree went out from Caesar Augustus that all the world should be enrolled. This was the first enrollment, when Quirinius was governor of Syria. And all went to be enrolled, each to his own city.

And Joseph also went up from Galilee, from the city of Nazareth, to Judea, to the city of David, which is called Bethlehem, because he was of the house and lineage of David, to be enrolled with Mary his betrothed, who was with child.

> *"I bring you good news of a great joy which will come to all the people; for to you is born this day in the city of David a Savior, who is the Christ the Lord."*
>
> — Luke 2:10–11 —

And while they were there, the time came for her to be delivered. And she gave birth to her first-born son and wrapped him swaddling cloths, and laid him in a manger, because there was no place for them in the inn.

And in that region there were shepherds out in the field, keeping watch over their flock by night.

And an angel of the Lord appeared to them, and the glory of the Lord shone around them, and they were filled with fear. And the angel said to them, "Be not afraid; for behold, I bring you good news of a great joy which will come to all the people; for to you is born this day in the city of David a Savior, who is Christ the Lord. And this will be a sign for you: you will find a baby wrapped in swaddling cloths and lying in a manger."

And suddenly there was with the angel a multitude of the heavenly host, praising God and saying,

"Glory to God in the highest, and on earth peace among men with whom he is pleased!"

TELL THE

No matter how many times we hear it, the story of the first Christmas should never grow old. The Season of Advent is meant to expand our hearts a little more and more each year so that we are capable of receiving a deeper understanding of the joy of Christmas, whether it is our fifth celebration or our hundredth.

LECTIO
What facts about the first Christmas did you already know?

MEDITATIO
Which details had you forgotten about or are new to you?

ORATIO
Jesus was born in a stable because there was no room for the Holy Family in the inn. Ask Jesus to forgive you for times you haven't made space for Him in your life.

CONTEMPLATIO
Imagine sitting in the field and hearing the angels sing on the night Jesus was born.

Jesus became a tiny baby, but the mystery is so big it can't fit inside of our heads! It's okay if it is hard to understand the Incarnation. Ask Jesus to help you get both your heart and your head ready for His arrival!

♦ Remember that Advent means "Coming" and refers to the coming of Christ in history, at the end of time, and in our own lives. How does Jesus come into your life each and every day?
♦ The shepherds were among the first people who knew Jesus had come into the world. What do you think the shepherds said and did when the angels appeared outside of Bethlehem?
♦ Is your heart ready for Jesus to come?

You probably have been spending a lot of time getting your home ready for Christmas—putting up decorations, baking cookies, and wrapping presents. But how have you been getting your heart ready? Make sure you plan for a little quiet time between now and Christmas Eve to soak in Jesus' presence in the midst of the excitement. May we always remember in a new way each year the great gift that Jesus is to each of us.

THE SEASON OF Christmas

The Light of the World has come!

All our waiting has been fulfilled, but not exactly in the way the world expected.

Instead of arriving as a mighty king surrounded with power, strength, and wealth, Jesus came into the world as a tiny newborn baby. Mary and Joseph could gather together and gaze down into the face of their Savior as they held Him in their arms. Can you imagine the awe they must have felt? The cave in Bethlehem was a piece of Heaven on earth that first Christmas.

We know that good things are meant to be shared, so it shouldn't surprise us that it wasn't long before the Holy Family welcomed others to the celebration. First, the angels gave the message that all of Heaven rejoiced with His birth. Then shepherds followed the light and found the Messiah that had been foretold by the prophets. The journey of the Wise Men revealed that Christ came for all people of all times.

This Christmas, we too can kneel by the manger in worship, adoring Jesus, the Newborn King.

"Each year as the Church recalls the Mystery of the Incarnation, She urges us to renew the memory of the great love God has shown to us."

ST. CHARLES BORROMEO

VISIO DIVINA FOR CHRISTMAS
The Nativity *by Federico Barocci*

The Nativity, *Federico Barocci, 1597*

Spend some time praying Visio Divina with this painting of the birth of Jesus. Use the same steps as Lectio Divina: Lectio, Meditatio, Oratio, Contemplatio. First, slowly examine the art, noticing details and how it tells a story. Then, think about the painting and make connections to what you already know. Finally, take a few minutes to pray about the image, asking God questions as well as listening to what He shares with you.

REFLECTION QUESTIONS

◆ What do you notice about the light and darkness in the painting?
◆ Is this the environment you would expect the King of the Universe to be born into?
◆ What do you imagine Mary is thinking about?

THE VISIT OF THE SHEPHERDS
The Feast of the Holy Family

LUKE 2:15–20

When the angels went away from them into heaven, the shepherds said to one another, "Let us go over to Bethlehem and see this thing that has happened, which the Lord has made known to us."

And they went with haste, and found Mary and Joseph, and the baby lying in a manger. And when they saw it they made known the saying which had been told them concerning this child; and all who heard it wondered at what the shepherds told them.

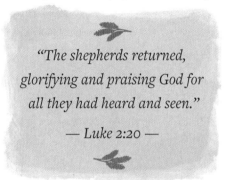

"The shepherds returned, glorifying and praising God for all they had heard and seen."

— Luke 2:20 —

But Mary kept all these things, pondering them in her heart. And the shepherds returned, glorifying and praising God for all they had heard and seen, as it had been told them.

TELL THE *Story*

We hear about shepherds all throughout the Bible—Abraham, Moses, and David were shepherds, Psalm 23 sings of the Lord our Shepherd, and Jesus teaches that He is the Good Shepherd.

The shepherds in our Christmas story are a little different, though. They are not famous, we don't know their names, and they might have even been outcasts from their communities. They lived outdoors alongside their sheep under the hot sun, rainy skies, and cold wind. They probably were dirty and grubby and spent a lot of time alone. And yet, these shepherds were the first ones invited to celebrate the birth of the King of the Universe alongside the Holy Family.

God loves each one of us and always has special plans for those who are humble and meek of heart. Like the shepherds who sacrificed their own comfort to care so gently for their sheep, Jesus comes into the world to save us, showing that each of us is loved and worthy.

- If there was a party for a newborn king, whom would you expect to be invited? Whom would you not expect?
- How did the Holy Family welcome the shepherds?
- How can we be more welcoming as a family?

 IT OUT

Just after Christmas, we celebrate the Feast of the Holy Family. We often talk the most about Joseph and Mary during the Advent and Christmas Season, but it's good to think about the fact that Jesus lived in their home in Nazareth until He was thirty years old. Thousands of family meals, hugs, stories, and prayers were shared between Jesus, Mary, and Joseph.

On this feast, thank God for your family and ask for His blessing on your home during the year to come using this prayer from Pope St. John Paul II: "May Jesus, Mary, and Joseph bless and protect all the world's families, so that within them may reign the serenity and joy, justice and peace that the newborn Christ has given as a gift to humanity."

LECTIO DIVINA

LECTIO
What did Mary do after the shepherds visited?

MEDITATIO
How can we follow Mary's example when we encounter Jesus in the Sacraments, while reading the Bible, or in prayer?

ORATIO
Ask Jesus to help you be like the shepherds, eager to come to meet Him.

CONTEMPLATIO
Close your eyes and picture being one of the shepherds, drawing close to the manger to peek at baby Jesus.

THE VISIT OF THE MAGI

Epiphany

MATTHEW 2:1–12

Now when Jesus was born in Bethlehem of Judea in the days of Herod the king, behold, Wise Men from the East came to Jerusalem, saying, "Where is he who has been born king of the Jews? For we have seen his star in the East, and have come to worship him."

When Herod the king heard this, he was troubled, and all Jerusalem with him; and assembling all the chief priests and scribes of the people, he inquired of them where the Christ was to be born. They told him, "In Bethlehem of Judea; for so it is written by the prophet:

'And you, O Bethlehem, in the land of Judah,
are by no means least among the rulers of Judah;
for from you shall come a ruler
who will govern my people Israel.'"

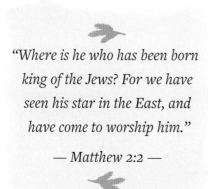

"Where is he who has been born king of the Jews? For we have seen his star in the East, and have come to worship him."

— Matthew 2:2 —

Then Herod summoned the Wise Men secretly and ascertained from them what time the star appeared; and he sent them to Bethlehem, saying, "Go and search diligently for the child, and when you have found him bring me word, that I too may come and worship him."

When they had heard the king they went their way; and behold, the star which they had seen in the East went before them, till it came to rest over the place where the child was. When they saw the star, they rejoiced exceedingly with great joy; and going into the house they saw the child with Mary his mother, and they fell down and worshiped him. Then, opening their treasures, they offered him gifts, gold and frankincense and myrrh.

And being warned in a dream not to return to Herod, they departed to their own country by another way.

TELL THE Story

Bringing gifts to a birthday party is a perfect way to celebrate—but Jesus got some interesting presents shortly after He was born. The Wise Men

What gifts did the Wise Men bring to baby Jesus?

MEDITATIO

How do those gifts connect to Jesus' life?

ORATIO

Ask Jesus to help you make your life a gift first to Him and then to others.

CONTEMPLATIO

Imagine kneeling at the manger next to Mary and Joseph.

who traveled from the East brought gold, frankincense, and myrrh, which are not exactly typical gifts for a baby! But those Magi knew that they weren't meeting just any baby; they were coming to see the newborn king of the Jews.

The gifts they brought tell us what they believed about Jesus: gold because He would rule as king, frankincense for His worship as high priest, and myrrh for His sacrifice that would save us.

The Wise Men had followed a star all the way to Bethlehem to find Jesus, traveling thousands of miles to honor the Messiah. Each Epiphany, we remember the journey that changed their hearts and showed us that Jesus is a gift for the whole world.

◆ What do you think the Wise Men's journey was like?
◆ If you could bring baby Jesus a gift, what would it be?
◆ The Wise Men departed from Bethlehem and went home "by another way." How are our lives meant to change when we come to know Jesus?

Live IT OUT

Epiphany is a perfect day to bless your home.

With a piece of chalk, write 20+C+M+B+21 (or current year) on or above your front door. The 2021 is for the year, and the C, M, and B represent the traditional names of the Wise Men: Caspar, Melchior, and Balthasar.

The CMB also stands for *"Christus mansionem benedicat,"* which is Latin for "May Christ bless this home." This is a perfect way to remind your family to pursue the virtue of hospitality. Just as the Holy Family welcomed the Wise Men, our homes are intended to be places of welcome.

THE SEASON OF Ordinary Time

After the excitement of Christmas, Ordinary Time can seem . . . well, ordinary. But it is anything but boring!

The name for Ordinary Time comes from the word "order" and signifies that the season has a pattern and structure. During Ordinary Time, we are called to grow in our love and knowledge of Christ, which is why the color of the season is green. This growth comes from making our faith part of everything we do, even during these "ordinary" days between Christmas and Easter.

There are two chunks of Ordinary Time in our liturgical year. The first one is fairly short and stretches from Epiphany until just before Lent. Depending on when Ash Wednesday falls, this part of Ordinary Time could be from four to nine weeks.

In this section of our book, we are going to focus on getting to know Jesus' early life and ministry. We will read a few stories about Jesus' own childhood, as well as His Baptism, first public miracle, and the call of the Disciples.

During the beginning of Ordinary Time, ask Jesus to draw you close to Him in the regular, everyday parts of your life. Look for Him in the ordinary, and you will find Him!

"Home life is the God-appointed training ground of human character, for from the home life of the child springs the maturity of manhood, either for good or for evil."

ARCHBISHOP FULTON J. SHEEN

VISIO DIVINA FOR ORDINARY TIME
The Baptism of Christ *by Francesco Trevisani*

The Baptism of Christ, *Francesco Trevisani, 1723*

Spend some time praying Visio Divina with this painting of Jesus' baptism in the Jordan River. Use the same steps as Lectio Divina: *Lectio, Meditatio, Oratio, Contemplatio*. First, slowly examine the art, noticing details and how it tells a story. Then, think about the painting and make connections to what you already know. Finally, take a few minutes to pray about the image, asking God questions as well as listening to what He shares with you.

REFLECTION QUESTIONS

- Can you find the Holy Trinity depicted in this painting?
- Looking at the far right, do you see Adam and Eve? Why do you think the artist included them in the background of this image of the baptism of Christ?
- Jesus' baptism in the Jordan River by St. John the Baptist marked the beginning of His public ministry and also gave the Church a model to follow for Baptism. Do you see any symbols of the Sacrament of Baptism in this artwork?

THE BAPTISM OF JESUS

The Baptism of the Lord

MARK 1:9–11

"You are my beloved Son; with you I am well pleased."

— *Mark 1:11* —

In those days Jesus came from Nazareth of Galilee and was baptized by John in the Jordan. And when he came up out of the water, immediately he saw the heavens opened and the Spirit descending upon him like a dove; and a voice came from heaven, "You are my beloved Son; with you I am well pleased."

TELL THE *Story*

After the weeks of waiting and preparing during Advent, and celebrating the birth of Jesus at Christmas, suddenly Jesus is all grown up in this reading during the first week of Ordinary Time!

It's not that Jesus' childhood isn't important (the Bible shares a few stories with us) but that the Church has us move right into another beginning, the beginning of Jesus' public ministry at His Baptism in the Jordan River. Jesus did not need to be baptized. He had not sinned. Jesus is God, and is sinless, but He was giving us an example to follow.

When you were baptized, you were washed clean of Original Sin, you became an adopted child of God, and you were welcomed into the Church. This Baptism, your first Sacrament, is the beginning of a Christian life following the model of Christ.

◆ Here at the start of Ordinary Time, we will hear stories of Jesus' teachings and miracles to help us follow in His footsteps. How do we follow Jesus during Ordinary Time?
◆ Do you know or remember anything about your own baptism?
◆ What are some ways we can be like Jesus today?

Live IT OUT

Just like you celebrate your birthday, it's also incredibly special to commemorate your Baptismal anniversary. If you don't know the date, check your family records or contact the church where you were baptized. A simple celebration involving lighting your Baptismal Candle (or another candle if it is not available), looking at pictures of your baptism, and making the Sign of the Cross when you pray (to recall how the Trinity was invoked at your baptism) can solidify the importance of this first Sacrament.

Reading the story of Jesus' Baptism and then connecting it to our own helps us remember that we are all made in God's image and likeness, and are called to bring Him into the world through all our thoughts, words, and actions.

LECTIO DIVINA

LECTIO
The Holy Trinity is present in this story. Can you find God the Father, God the Son, and God the Holy Spirit?

MEDITATIO
What would it have been like to witness Jesus' Baptism?

ORATIO
Ask God to help you live out the graces of your baptism throughout your whole life.

CONTEMPLATIO
Listen to God the Father saying to you, "You are my child; with you I am well pleased."

THE PRESENTATION IN THE TEMPLE
The 2nd Week of Ordinary Time

LUKE 2:22–38

And when the time came for their purification according to the law of Moses, they brought him up to Jerusalem to present him to the Lord (as it is written in the law of the Lord, "Every male that opens the womb shall be called holy to the Lord") and to offer a sacrifice according to what is said in the law of the Lord, "a pair of turtledoves, or two young pigeons."

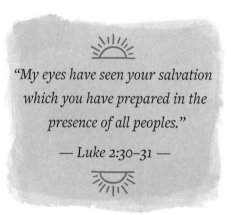

"My eyes have seen your salvation which you have prepared in the presence of all peoples."

— Luke 2:30–31 —

Now there was a man in Jerusalem, whose name was Simeon, and this man was righteous and devout, looking for the consolation of Israel, and the Holy Spirit was upon him. And it had been revealed to him by the Holy Spirit that he should not see death before he had seen the Lord's Christ. And inspired by the Spirit he came into the temple; and when the parents brought in the child Jesus, to do for him according to the custom of the law, he took him up in his arms and blessed God and said,

"Lord, now let your servant depart in peace,
according to your word;
for my eyes have seen your salvation
which you have prepared in the presence of all peoples,
a light for revelation to the Gentiles,
and for glory to your people Israel."

And his father and his mother marveled at what was said about him; and Simeon blessed them and said to Mary his mother,

"Behold, this child is set for the fall and rising of many in Israel,
and for a sign that is spoken against
(and a sword will pierce through your own soul also),
that thoughts out of many hearts may be revealed."

And there was a prophetess, Anna, the daughter of Phanuel, of the tribe of Asher; she was of a great age, having lived with her husband seven years from her virginity, and as a widow till she was eighty-four. She did not depart from the temple, worshiping with fasting and prayer night and day. And coming up at that very hour she gave thanks to God, and spoke of him to all who were looking for the redemption of Jerusalem.

LECTIO DIVINA

LECTIO
What words from Simeon's prayer are most special to you?

MEDITATIO
How do Simeon and Anna show their belief that Jesus is God?

ORATIO
Pray to be like Simeon and Anna, seeing Jesus and praising Him.

CONTEMPLATIO
What would it be like to wait in the temple with Simeon and Anna?

TELL THE *Story*

Imagine praying in your church for a long time for something God has promised you. Then a young couple walks in with a baby and you *know* that He is the Messiah you've been waiting for!

Back during the Season of Advent, we read that the Israelites had been waiting for thousands of years for the Savior to come. Simeon and Anna were holy Jews who spent so much time praying and learning about God that they were able to recognize that the Messiah was baby Jesus when Mary and Joseph presented Him in the temple.

◆ How can we open our hearts to see Jesus in the people around us?
◆ What prophecies (predictions from God) did Simeon make about Jesus?
◆ How did they come true?

Live IT OUT

One powerful part of Simeon's prophetic words is his foresight into the suffering that the Holy Family would endure. Although we may not understand why God called Jesus and His Holy Family to endure suffering, all of Jesus' earthly actions make more sense with His Crucifixion and Resurrection in mind.

Simeon's message to Mary also reminds us that suffering is not individualized in the Body of Christ. When one of us suffers, we are united with them and can bring them to the comforting arms of Jesus. How you can practically help those who are suffering—whether with support, comfort, or prayers?

THE HOLY FAMILY IN NAZARETH
The 3rd Week of Ordinary Time

LUKE 2:39-40

And when they had performed everything according to the law of the Lord, they returned to Galilee, to their own city, Nazareth. And the child grew and became strong, filled with wisdom; and the favor of God was upon him.

"They returned into Galilee, to their own city, Nazareth."

— *Luke 2:39* —

TELL THE

We know Jesus grew up in Nazareth, but the Bible doesn't share many details about the life of the Holy Family. Based on what we believe about Jesus, as well as the virtue of the Blessed Virgin Mary and St. Joseph, their home must have been filled with more love than we can imagine.

But it also was the home of three real people, so it can be edifying to picture Jesus playing with toys Joseph made for Him, or Mary washing the dishes after dinner, or St. Joseph cleaning up his carpentry shop after a long day of work. The love the Holy Family had for one another made this quiet, ordinary time in their lives a great gift.

Your home too can be a place of joy. Work on looking for ways to show love to your family even in the normal, everyday actions of playing, cleaning, eating, and praying.

- ◆ How do you think Jesus' childhood was similar to yours?
- ◆ How might it have been different?
- ◆ Pretend you could spend one day with Jesus when He was the same age as you. What would you do during your day together?

IT OUT

The Holy Family gives us a glimpse of the ideal domestic church. Archbishop Fulton J. Sheen said, "Home life is the God-appointed training ground of human character, for from the home life of the child springs the maturity of manhood, either for good or for evil." The growth of Jesus in the home of Mary and Joseph presents a model to follow in every Christian home.

While the Bible provides few details about the quiet years in Nazareth, we can read about God's plans for the family and the role of parents and children all throughout Scripture. Under the guidance of the Holy Family, consider how you can continue to develop a culture of faith in your home as you grow into the next generation of followers of Christ.

LECTIO DIVINA

LECTIO
What word about Jesus' childhood stands out to you?

MEDITATIO
What types of things do you think Jesus learned from Mary and Joseph? What did they learn from Him?

ORATIO
Pray for your own family, that together you will live out the mission God sets before you.

CONTEMPLATIO
Think about cooking in the kitchen with Mary or working alongside Joseph.

THE FINDING OF JESUS IN THE TEMPLE

The 4th Week of Ordinary Time

LUKE 2:41–52

Now his parents went to Jerusalem every year at the feast of the Passover. And when he was twelve years old, they went up according to custom; and when the feast was ended, as they were returning, the boy Jesus stayed behind in Jerusalem.

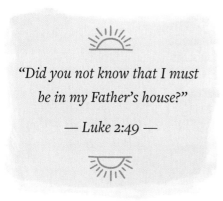

"Did you not know that I must be in my Father's house?"

— *Luke 2:49* —

His parents did not know it, but supposing him to be in the company they went a day's journey, and they sought him among their kinsfolk and acquaintances; and when they did not find him, they returned to Jerusalem, seeking him.

After three days they found him in the temple, sitting among the teachers, listening to them and asking them questions; and all who heard him were amazed at his understanding and his answers.

And when they saw him they were astonished; and his mother said to him, "Son, why have you treated us so? Behold, your father and I have been looking for you anxiously."

And he said to them, "How is it that you sought me? Did you not know that I must be in my Father's house?" And they did not understand the saying which he spoke to them. And he went down with them and came to Nazareth, and was obedient to them; and his mother kept all these things in her heart. And Jesus increased in wisdom and in stature, and in favor with God and man.

TELL THE *Story*

Have you ever gotten lost? Maybe you stepped away from your dad in the grocery store or couldn't find your mom while playing in the park. Even if it was only for a moment, it can be scary to feel separated from your family.

Mary and Joseph thought they had lost Jesus in this story! They were traveling in a group and each thought Jesus was somewhere with their traveling companions. By the time they found Him back in the temple in Jerusalem, it had been three days. Imagine how worried they must have been!

LECTIO
What surprised you about this story?

MEDITATIO
What emotions do you think Mary and Joseph felt during this experience?

ORATIO
Pray to grow in the virtue of obedience.

CONTEMPLATIO
Ask Jesus to show you how to "keep all these things in your heart" just like Mary.

But remember, God never wants us to be filled with fear. He desires us to trust and listen to Him. Jesus wasn't really lost . . . He had just stayed to teach in the temple, His Father's house.

♦ The three days the Blessed Virgin Mary and St. Joseph couldn't find Jesus remind us of another important three days that will happen later in the Bible. Do you remember how long Jesus lay in the tomb after His death on the Cross? Three days!

♦ Jesus' followers were sad and afraid because they thought they had lost Him forever. But on the morning of the third day, Jesus rose from the grave and showed us that we can never be separated from Him. How does the Finding in the Temple point us to the hope of the Resurrection on Easter Sunday?

♦ How does this story help us to trust all of God's promises?

Live IT OUT

It can be surprising to read at the end of the Finding in the Temple that the Holy Family returned to Nazareth and Jesus "was obedient to them." Even though He is the Second Person of the Trinity, truly God, and the Savior of the World, the child Jesus was obedient to His mother and foster father. This model of obedience is a lesson to us all.

Obedience is not merely a hierarchy of power, but an act of humility and love for the other. Growing in the virtue of obedience in your home or classroom is a mutual gift for both children and adults. Pray together this week to grow in this virtue after the model of the Holy Family.

THE WORD OF GOD

JOHN 1:1-5

In the beginning was the Word, and the Word was with God, and the Word was God. He was in the beginning with God; all things were made through him, and without him was not anything made that was made. In him was life, and the life was the light of men. The light shines in the darkness, and the darkness has not overcome it.

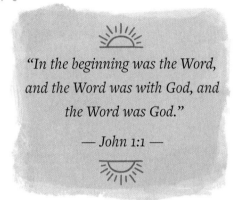

"In the beginning was the Word, and the Word was with God, and the Word was God."

— John 1:1 —

TELL THE Story

The Bible uses all types of language to teach us about God. Sometimes we read poetry or songs; other times the Bible gives us lists of advice or wisdom from the prophets. The Gospels are the first four books of the New Testament, and they share the stories of Jesus on earth. Usually the Gospels are in a narrative form, which means the story has people, places, and events.

Our reading today from the beginning of the Gospel of John isn't a typical story about Jesus, but that doesn't mean it isn't worth reading. St. John starts with a more poetic look at who Jesus is, calling Him the Word. This name is used again in the Book of Revelation, reminding us that Jesus always has been and always will be.

◆ How does our world use words? Think about how we learn words, communicate with words, and create with words.
◆ What do you think the name "Word of God" means?
◆ Why did St. John use this title for Jesus?

Live IT OUT

We use the title "Word of God" as a name for Jesus, but it also is another name for the Holy Bible. We believe that Sacred Scripture is inspired, meaning that while the books were recorded by human writers, God Himself is the author of the message. Because of this, the Bible is more than just a book. It is a message from God to His people in every age and place.

You can have many Bibles in your home for personal study and children's Bibles and storybooks to read, but it can be powerful to also have a special family Bible in a place of honor. That Holy Bible might be on a small home altar, special shelf, or other central location in your home.

Having the Word of God present in your home invites your family into personal prayer right within your domestic church.

LECTIO DIVINA

LECTIO
These verses are a description of Jesus. Read them one more time and listen to what the words teach you about Him.

MEDITATIO
What symbols are used in this passage? What do they tell you about who Jesus is?

ORATIO
Ask Jesus to show you Himself through the Word of God, the Bible.

CONTEMPLATIO
Choose one word from this passage. Close your eyes and focus on connecting that word to the life of Christ.

VISIO DIVINA FOR ORDINARY TIME
The Wedding Feast at Cana *by Tintoretto*

The Wedding Feast at Cana, *Tintoretto, 1545*

Spend some time praying Visio Divina with this painting of Jesus' first miracle: the Wedding at Cana. Use the same steps as Lectio Divina: *Lectio, Meditatio, Oratio, Contemplatio*. First, slowly examine the art, noticing details and how it tells a story. Then, think about the painting and make connections to what you already know. Finally, take a few minutes to pray about the image, asking God questions as well as listening to what He shares with you.

REFLECTION QUESTIONS

- The Wedding at Cana was where Jesus performed His first public miracle. Do you know what happened in this story? (If not, you can skip ahead to the reading for the 6th Week of Ordinary Time!)
- What part of the painting does your eye notice first?
- Where is Mary in relation to Jesus? What is happening?
- How would you have reacted if you had witnessed one of Jesus' miracles?

THE WEDDING AT CANA
The 6th Week of Ordinary Time

JOHN 2:1–11

On the third day there was a marriage at Cana in Galilee, and the mother of Jesus was there; Jesus also was invited to the marriage, with his disciples.

When the wine failed, the mother of Jesus said to him, "They have no wine." And Jesus said to her, "O woman, what have you to do with me? My hour has not yet come."

"His mother said to the servants, 'Do whatever he tells you.'"

— John 2:5 —

His mother said to the servants, "Do whatever he tells you." Now six stone jars were standing there, for the Jewish rites of purification, each holding twenty or thirty gallons. Jesus said to them, "Fill the jars with water." And they filled them up to the brim. He said to them, "Now draw some out, and take it to the steward of the feast." So they took it.

When the steward of the feast tasted the water now become wine, and did not know where it came from (though the servants who had drawn the water knew), the steward of the feast called the bridegroom and said to him, "Every man serves the good wine first; and when men have drunk freely, then the poor wine; but you have kept the good wine until now."

This, the first of his signs, Jesus did at Cana in Galilee, and manifested his glory; and his disciples believed in him.

BARTOLOMEO DI
ANTONIO PICCIVOLI
ANNO·DÑI·M·D·C·XIII·

TELL THE

Have you ever run out of something important? What if you were short on food or drink at a party you were hosting—how would you feel?

In this story, Jesus and Mary were guests at a wedding when the hosts ran out of wine. A wedding is always an important celebration and a time for the families of the bride and groom to show great hospitality to their friends and family. By not having enough, the hosts might feel that they had disappointed their guests and the party would come to an end. Mary knew Jesus could fix the problem, so she asked for His help—even though that meant He would have to perform a miracle.

Mary always followed God's will, so after asking Jesus, she told the servers to listen and to do whatever Jesus asked of them. Mary's example is an important model for us to follow. We can always ask Jesus for what we need, and then we should listen and obey Him. Wonderful things will happen when we follow the will of Jesus!

- What do you think the guests were thinking when they witnessed this miracle?
- By changing the water into wine, others would start to know that Jesus was no ordinary guy. He chose to reveal this mystery to us at the Wedding at Cana, which also shows us the importance of the Sacrament of Matrimony. Do you know any couples preparing to receive this Sacrament? You can pray for them, as well as for any married couples you know.
- We might not have been able to witness the miracle at the Wedding at Cana, but it reminds us of other amazing things Jesus came to do. Remember that at the Last Supper Jesus was drinking wine with the apostles when He told them that the wine would actually become His Blood! We experience this miracle in the Eucharist every time we attend Mass.

IT OUT

The story of the Wedding at Cana is often used as a background on Catholic devotion to Mary. Why do we honor Mary, look to her example, and ask for her prayers? Simply, we love Mary because Christ loved her first.

Out of all creation, God asked Mary to bring His Son into the world. Mary's "fiat," her yes to the will of the Father, marks her as the New Eve and shows that she plays a crucial role in salvation history. Her whole life was spent glorifying God and doing His will. We see this in her response at the Annunciation and in her instructions to the servers at the Wedding at Cana. Mary tells us to "do whatever He tells you" and helps us follow by example. At His death on the Cross, Jesus gave the Church His mother

LECTIO DIVINA

LECTIO
How did the people at the wedding react to what happened?

MEDITATIO
What would you have thought if you witnessed this miracle?

ORATIO
Ask Mary to help you always do what Jesus tells you.

CONTEMPLATIO
Think about something important you feel you don't have "enough" of in your life. Ask Jesus to turn the water into wine and give you everything you need.

as our own, and she continues that maternal role from Heaven.

Mary always leads us directly to her Son. In your home, you can grow in devotion to Our Blessed Mother by displaying a picture or statue of Mary. Much like we hang up photos of our family members, having images of Mary and the saints around us reminds us of our family in Heaven.

We only worship God, but Mary and the saints who have gone before us model for us how to live out our faith in God in the world. We look to their example and ask for their prayers, just as we would ask for the prayers of our friends and family here on earth.

THE CALL OF THE DISCIPLES
The 7th Week of Ordinary Time

MATTHEW 4:18-22

As he walked by the Sea of Galilee, he saw two brothers, Simon who is called Peter and Andrew his brother, casting a net into the sea; for they were fishermen. And he said to them, "Follow me, and I will make you fishers of men." Immediately they left their nets and followed him.

And going on from there he saw two other brothers, James the son of Zebedee and John his brother, in the boat with Zebedee their father, mending their nets, and he called them. Immediately they left the boat and their father, and followed him.

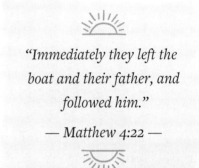

"Immediately they left the boat and their father, and followed him."

— Matthew 4:22 —

TELL THE Story

Change can be hard. We often choose to do things that we are familiar with because they are comfortable.

Peter, Andrew, James, and John made a big change in this story. They had a predictable life as fishermen with their boats and nets and routine. But Jesus comes to call them to something even better. He asks them to follow Him, leaving behind their old way of life.

Their encounter with Jesus must have been powerful enough to erase all fear and give them the courage to leave their boats and families and follow Him. And the apostles went on to walk with Jesus during His public ministry and then out to tell the Good News as His witnesses.

◆ Do you think change is difficult, or do you think it is fun?
◆ What would be some good reasons to make a big change in your life?
◆ What else do you think Jesus said or did that day when he called the apostles?

LIVE IT OUT

Never in a million years could we have predicted whom Jesus would chose as His closest followers. Fishermen, a tax collector, a zealot . . . none of them famous, none of them rich, none of them powerful. Jesus called a group of simple, working-class men to first become His friends and then to change the world.

A vocation is a calling from God. We often think of this word only in connection to vocations like marriage or the priesthood, but it also means the work that God places before us each day.

It's never too early to begin listening to God's voice. The virtue of prudence helps us discern right from wrong in any given situation and choose to do it. By obeying God and acting prudently in small decisions, we are more prepared to listen to Him in the big decisions. Using the example of the call of the apostles, talk as a family about making good choices and discerning God's will.

LECTIO DIVINA

LECTIO
Which of the apostles do we meet in this story?

MEDITATIO
What did they do when Jesus called them?

ORATIO
Pray about listening well to Jesus.

CONTEMPLATIO
Think about what Jesus means when He says "fishers of men."

THE SEASON OF Lent

Ash Wednesday is the start of forty days in which we are called to grow closer to Jesus with focused effort. The Church guides us through the Season of Lent, and our path is marked with prayer, fasting, and almsgiving. We pray, fast, and give all the time, but we try to increase the quality and quantity during Lent.

The Lenten Season is a perfect opportunity to challenge ourselves, with the help of the Holy Spirit, to grow in virtue. A virtue is a habit of choosing the good in any situation. There are many virtues, but they all stem from the Theological Virtues of faith, hope, and love or the Cardinal Virtues of prudence, justice, temperance, and fortitude. The reflections for each week of Lent will include a connection to a virtue for you to put into practice during Lent.

The first mark of Lent is prayer. Prayer is communication with God, both talking to Him and listening. Spending time reading the Bible, saying memorized prayers, using a tool like the Rosary, and writing in a journal can all be great ways to pray. There are many different ways to pray, but it is important to talk to God every day.

The second mark of Lent is fasting. When we fast, we give up something that can be good, like our favorite food, television show, or toy, and we choose to give them up because we love God more. Fasting makes room in our heart to notice the suffering of others around us. We can fast from something good during Lent and then celebrate by enjoying it again at Easter, or we can work on giving up a bad habit totally. Fasting helps us to focus on what really matters, which are things of Heaven and not of earth.

Giving is the third mark of Lent. We are always called to be generous, and Lent is a great opportunity to find ways to be more giving with our time, talent, and treasure, both to those close to us as well as to the whole world. How do you plan to pray, fast, and give during this Season of Lent?

"The Cross is the school of love."
ST. MAXIMILIAN KOLBE

VISIO DIVINA FOR LENT
The Crucifixion *by Diego Velázquez*

The Crucifixion, *Diego Velázquez, 1632*

Spend some time praying Visio Divina with this painting of Jesus' Crucifixion. Use the same steps as Lectio Divina: *Lectio, Meditatio, Oratio, Contemplatio*. First, slowly examine the art, noticing details and how it tells a story. Then, think about the painting and make connections to what you already know. Finally, take a few minutes to pray about the image, asking God questions as well as listening to what He shares with you.

REFLECTION QUESTIONS

- What details do you notice in this image of the Crucifixion?
- What do you think about the artist's choice to make the background solid black?
- Sit for a few minutes in quiet looking at this picture or a crucifix in your home, classroom, or church.

THE TEMPTATION IN THE DESERT

The 1st Week of Lent

MATTHEW 4:1–11

Then Jesus was led up by the Spirit into the wilderness to be tempted by the devil. And he fasted forty days and forty nights, and afterward he was hungry. And the tempter came and said to him, "If you are the Son of God, command these stones to become loaves of bread." But he answered, "It is written,

'Man shall not live by bread alone,
but by every word that proceeds from the mouth of God.'"

Then the devil took him to the holy city, and set him on the pinnacle of the temple, and said to him, "If you are the Son of God, throw yourself down; for it is written,

'He will give his angels charge of you,' and 'On their hands they will bear you up, lest you strike your foot against a stone.'"

Jesus said to him, "Again it is written, 'You shall not tempt the Lord your God.'" Again, the devil took him to a very high mountain, and showed him all the kingdoms of the world and the glory of them; and he said to him, "All these I will give you, if you will fall down and worship me." Then Jesus said to him, "Begone, Satan! for it is written,

"'You shall worship the Lord your God and him only shall you serve.'"

— Matthew 4:10 —

'You shall worship the Lord your God
and him only shall you serve.'"

Then the devil left him, and behold, angels came and ministered to him.

TELL THE *Story*

Just after Jesus' Baptism in the Jordan River, He was led into the desert by the Holy Spirit and fasted for forty days and nights. Jesus was fully God but also fully man, so He must have been tired and hungry. At the end of the forty days, Satan tried to tempt Jesus to deny God and worship the devil instead.

A temptation is when we struggle to choose between something good, which often seems challenging, and something evil, which usually seems easier. Jesus was tempted by hunger, greed, and pride. During the Season of Lent, we are given the chance to reject those three temptations through prayer, fasting, and almsgiving. Prayer teaches us to give up pride and rely on God. Fasting helps us see that the things that we hunger for are less important than our Lord. Almsgiving causes us to focus not on our greed but on the needs of others.

Every Lent is an invitation to walk in the desert with Jesus, where He will help us pray, fast, and give just like He did.

- What question would you ask Jesus when He came back from the desert?
- Jesus' time in the desert inspires us to pray, fast, and give as a way to overcome temptation. Which mark of Lent is hardest for you: prayer, fasting, or almsgiving?
- We know making sacrifices is difficult. Are you at your best when you are tired and hungry? How can you work to be patient with others even when you are uncomfortable?

IT OUT

Make a practical plan for Lent with ways for each member of your family to pray, fast, and give. It can be meaningful to connect your plans for prayer, fasting, and almsgiving to the virtues of faith, hope, and love, which guide the purpose behind our Lenten sacrifices and challenges. Write your commitments down and tuck them in your Bible or post them on the fridge.

During Lent, we journey toward the Cross. Jesus and the saints who've gone before us can act as our guides.

St. Maximilian Kolbe was a Franciscan priest from Poland who spent his life teaching about Jesus. He wrote newspapers, created magazines, broadcast a radio show, and inspired Catholics to practice their faith richly and faithfully. But Fr. Maximilian lived in a time when speaking out for faith and values was not allowed by the government, and eventually he was arrested and sent to Auschwitz, a concentration camp. There he continued to minister by helping the camp prisoners, and eventually offered his own life to save another man even though he was a stranger. St. Maximilian Kolbe's life can serve as a powerful example for how the sacrifices of Lent can teach us to follow Christ.

LECTIO DIVINA

LECTIO
What were the three temptations Jesus faced in the desert?

MEDITATIO
What was Jesus teaching us through His actions and words during His forty days in the desert?

ORATIO
Ask Jesus to be with you when you face hard decisions.

CONTEMPLATIO
Ponder how quiet the desert would have been. Listen to what God has to say to you.

THE PREACHING OF JOHN THE BAPTIST

The 2nd Week of Lent

MARK 1:2-8

As it is written in Isaiah the prophet,
"Behold, I send my messenger before your face,
who shall prepare your way;
the voice of one crying in the wilderness:
Prepare the way of the Lord,
make his paths straight—"

"After me comes he who is mightier than I."

— Mark 1:7 —

John the Baptist appeared in the wilderness, preaching a baptism of repentance for the forgiveness of sins. And there went out to him all the country of Judea, and all the people of Jerusalem; and they were baptized by him in the river Jordan, confessing their sins.

Now John was clothed with camel's hair, and had a leather belt around his waist, and ate locusts and wild honey. And he preached saying, "After me comes he who is mightier than I, the thong of whose sandals I am not worthy to stoop down and untie. I have baptized you with water; but he will baptize you with the Holy Spirit."

TELL THE *Story*

Thirty years before this story, we met John the Baptist, but he was just a tiny baby! Remember the Visitation when Mary went to see Elizabeth and Zechariah, and both the Blessed Virgin Mary and St. Elizabeth were expecting miraculous babies? Mary's baby was Jesus and Elizabeth's baby was St. John the Baptist!

Jesus and John were related and probably spent time together while they were growing up. Now as an adult, John goes out to the desert to pray and grow close to God. His interesting clothing was a sign that he was a prophet like Elijah in the Old Testament. A prophet is someone who shared a message with God's people, and John's voice and his mission were to point others' attention to Jesus.

We hear a lot about deserts at the beginning of Lent. A desert is not a bad place, but it can symbolize being away from the normal comforts of life.

LECTIO DIVINA

LECTIO
How is John the Baptist described?

MEDITATIO
Why do you think people traveled to meet St. John the Baptist?

ORATIO
Ask Jesus to help you be His messenger just like John.

CONTEMPLATIO
What will help you focus on Jesus this Lent?

In the Bible, there are many stories about people seeking to connect with God and to disconnect from the world. St. John the Baptist certainly put this into practice as he spent time in the wilderness and called people to look for the coming of the Messiah.

- How can you spend time in the "desert" this Lent?
- What do you think you are being called to disconnect from?
- How can you use your voice to point others to Jesus?

Live IT OUT

A perfect virtue to cultivate during Lent is temperance because it helps us to fast. Temperance is using moderation in the way you enjoy good things like food or your favorite hobby.

What are some ways you tend to waste time during the day? What are some of your favorite hobbies/shows/foods? Could you make a sacrifice and give up one of them for Lent? Do you have any bad habits that you want to work on breaking? How could giving up one thing make room for something better?

THE AGONY IN THE GARDEN

The 3rd Week of Lent

MATTHEW 26:36–46

Then Jesus went with them to a place called Gethsemane, and he said to his disciples, "Sit here, while I go over there and pray." And taking with him Peter and the two sons of Zebedee, he began to be sorrowful and troubled. Then he said to them, "My soul is very sorrowful, even to death; remain here, and watch with me."

And going a little farther he fell on his face and prayed, "My Father, if it be possible, let this chalice pass from me; nevertheless, not as I will, but as you will."

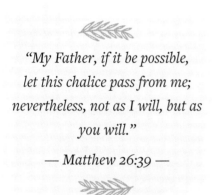

"My Father, if it be possible, let this chalice pass from me; nevertheless, not as I will, but as you will."

— Matthew 26:39 —

And he came to the disciples and found them sleeping; and he said to Peter, "So, could you not watch with me one hour? Watch and pray that you may not enter into temptation; the spirit indeed is willing, but the flesh is weak."

Again, for the second time, he went away and prayed, "My Father, if this cannot pass unless I drink it, your will be done."

And again he came and found them sleeping, for their eyes were heavy. So, leaving them again, he went away and prayed for the third time, saying the same words.

Then he came to the disciples and said to them, "Are you still sleeping and taking your rest? Behold, the hour is at hand, and the Son of man is betrayed into the hands of sinners. Rise, let us be going; see, my betrayer is at hand."

TELL THE

Jesus often went off alone to pray. As the time for His Crucifixion drew near, He spent time in solitude seeking the will of His Father.

The garden in this story reminds us of the garden we hear about at the beginning of the Bible, the Garden of Eden. Here God created Adam and Eve and gave them everything they needed. But the first man and woman were tempted to not trust God. Instead of seeking His will, they followed what they wanted to do and ate from the forbidden tree. Because of their sin, they had to leave the perfect garden, now surviving by their sweat among the thorns.

Even though Adam and Eve didn't trust Him, God promised to send a Redeemer to save them and bring them back into communion with Him. Thousands of years later in another garden, the Son of God sought the will of His Father and redeemed us with His sweat and blood. He wore a Crown of Thorns and was nailed to a tree to save us and bring us back into the family of God. The Bible is one continuous story that all finds fulfillment in Jesus Christ.

- How do you see Jesus following God's will during the Agony in the Garden?
- How do you usually handle suffering? In what ways could you try to follow Jesus' model?
- Jesus is called the New Adam because He fulfilled God's promises first made in the Garden of Eden. Can you think of any other connections between Jesus and Adam?

LECTIO

How did Jesus pray while He was in the Garden of Gethsemane?

MEDITATIO

What did Peter, James, and John do while Jesus prayed? What could they have done differently?

ORATIO

Ask Jesus to help you pray in times of suffering.

CONTEMPLATIO

Imagine sitting next to Jesus in the garden and praying with Him during His agony.

Live IT OUT

The virtue of self-control enables us to consider more than our immediate desires when making decisions. Self-control can protect us from committing sin and can also help us prioritize what is best over what is just good. Adam and Eve did not use self-control when they chose to ignore God's plan. They didn't trust that His will was better. Jesus demonstrated self-control in the Garden of Gethsemane and gave us an example of the strength of prayer in difficult situations. Self-control is a gate to growth in other virtues. During Lent, practicing little "nos" and "yeses" strengthens our self-control muscles so we are ready when big temptations occur.

As Jesus prayed in the Garden of Gethsemane, he asked the apostles if they couldn't watch one hour with Him. That call to an hour of prayer is one of the origins of the Catholic devotion of a Holy Hour. In Adoration, we pray with Jesus visible in the Blessed Sacrament. We don't have to give an hour, especially when we are bringing our little brothers and sisters to Adoration, but it is always a precious gift to stop into an Adoration chapel or unlocked church to spend even a few minutes with Jesus.

How would you like to grow in prayer this Lent? What is your favorite way to pray? What is a type of prayer you would like to learn or try? When during your day do you need to add in more prayer? When you wake up? Little prayers during the school day? Before bed? How do you desire to grow in prayer during Lent?

THE SCOURGING AT THE PILLAR
The 4th Week of Lent

MATTHEW 27:22–26

Pilate said to them, "Then what shall I do with Jesus who is called Christ?" They all said, "Let him be crucified." And he said, "Why, what evil has he done?" But they shouted all the more, "Let him be crucified."

So when Pilate saw that he was gaining nothing, but rather that a riot was beginning, he took water and washed his hands before the crowd, saying, "I am innocent of this righteous man's blood; see to it yourselves." And all the people answered, "His blood be on us and on our children!" Then he released for them Barabbas, and having scourged Jesus, delivered him to be crucified.

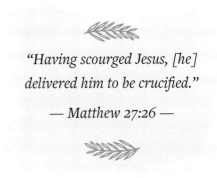

"Having scourged Jesus, [he] delivered him to be crucified."

— *Matthew 27:26* —

TELL THE

The Scourging at the Pillar is a hard story to read. We know that Jesus was innocent, so it is sad that people wanted Him to be punished. Jesus suffered through the scourging because He loves us. He wants to give us new life, and His Passion, Death, and Resurrection open up the gates of Heaven for us.

Jesus models the virtue of perseverance in His actions during Holy Week. Perseverance helps us to not give up when faced with challenges and keeps our focus on what matters most. Perseverance can also fill us with strength to make sacrifices for the sake of others.

One mark of Lent is almsgiving. Sharing generously is a way of showing our trust in God. We can help take care of others because we believe that God will take care of us. Even in the midst of difficult circumstances, and maybe more so in those times, our generosity helps us to persevere in following God's will and loving Him and our neighbor.

◆ What are some ways you could be more generous with your belongings?
◆ Who is someone that has shown generosity to you?
◆ What are some ways you could be more generous with your time?
◆ How would you like to grow in generosity this Lent?

IT OUT

Everything Christ did was to show us His love and to lead us to Heaven. Zélie Martin understood the virtues of perseverance and generosity.

Zélie owned a successful lace making business in France in the nineteenth century. She was a wife and mom of nine children, but sadly four of her children died when they were very young. The five daughters who lived to adulthood all became religious sisters, and one of them you probably know well: St. Thérèse of Lisieux! Zélie and her husband Louis prioritized their faith and followed God's will for their family. Sts. Zélie and Louis were the first married couple to be canonized together in modern times.

LECTIO DIVINA

LECTIO
How did Jesus show the virtue of perseverance during His trial?

MEDITATIO
Why did the crowd reject Jesus as the Messiah?

ORATIO
Ask Jesus to help you be generous in your thoughts, words, and actions.

CONTEMPLATIO
Think about God's great mercy and how He forgives our sins.

THE CROWNING WITH THORNS

The 5th Week of Lent

MARK 15:16–20

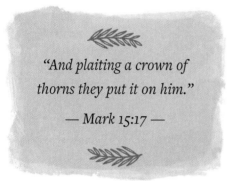

"And plaiting a crown of thorns they put it on him."

— Mark 15:17 —

And the soldiers led him away inside the palace (that is, the praetorium); and they called together the whole battalion. And they clothed him in a purple cloak, and plaiting a crown of thorns they put it on him. And they began to salute him, "Hail, King of the Jews!" And they struck his head with a reed, and spat upon him, and they knelt down in homage to him.

And when they had mocked him, they stripped him of the purple cloak, and put his own clothes on him. And they led him out to crucify him.

TELL THE Story

Jesus is our King. He rules over Heaven and earth, but not in the way we often think of the kings we read about in fairy tales or history books.

When Jesus walked on earth, He did not sit on a throne in a castle or eat at fancy banquets with the rich and famous or wear a crown of gold and jewels. Instead, Jesus sat on grassy hills and in fishing boats to teach His followers and ate simple meals with outcasts and sinners. And near the end of His earthly life, He wore a Crown of Thorns which was meant to mock and humiliate Him.

The soldiers' goal was to make fun of Jesus and His lack of power, but they had no idea that he was about to do the most powerful things ever—rise from the dead and save us from our sins. That is what makes Him our King and means that the Crown of Thorns is not a symbol of defeat, but one of victory.

◆ Have you ever been made fun of for doing the right thing?
◆ How did you feel? How did you stay strong?
◆ In what ways do you show the world that Jesus is the King of your life?

LECTIO DIVINA

LECTIO
In what ways did the soldiers make fun of Jesus?

MEDITATIO
How do you feel about the way Jesus was treated?

ORATIO
Pray for those who are persecuted for their faith.

CONTEMPLATIO
What do you think of when you see Jesus wearing a Crown of Thorns instead of a crown of gold?

Meekness does not mean that you are nothing. It actually means that you are so valuable that no external circumstances or opinions can change who you are. Being meek allows us to accept what is happening around us because we know our dignity and worth come from being made in God's image and likeness. Even in suffering, maybe especially in suffering, this humble virtue helps us keep our eyes on Heaven. Christ proves that during the Crowning with Thorns.

During Lent, look for opportunities to practice the virtue of meekness following the model of Jesus.

THE CARRYING OF THE CROSS
The 6th Week of Lent

MATTHEW 27: 32–44

As they were marching out, they came upon a man of Cyrene, Simon by name; this man they compelled to carry his cross.

And when they came to a place called Golgotha (which means the place of a skull), they offered him wine to drink, mingled with gall; but when he tasted it, he would not drink it. And when they had crucified him, they divided his garments among them by casting lots; then they sat down and kept watch over him there. And over his head they put the charge against him, which read, "This is Jesus the King of the Jews."

Then two robbers were crucified with him, one on the right and one on the left. And those who passed by derided him, wagging their heads and saying, "You who would destroy the temple and build it in three days, save yourself! If you are the Son of God, come down from the cross." So also the chief priests, with the scribes and elders, mocked him, saying, "He saved others; he cannot save himself. He is the King of Israel; let him come down now from the cross, and we will believe in him. He trusts in God; let God deliver him now, if he desires him; for he said, 'I am the Son of God.'" And the robbers who were crucified with him also reviled him in the same way.

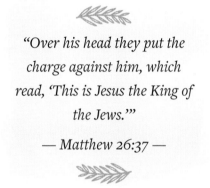

"Over his head they put the charge against him, which read, 'This is Jesus the King of the Jews.'"

— *Matthew 26:37* —

TELL THE

Lent might be feeling long this week. Our Lenten sacrifices sometimes seem more and more difficult the longer we try to keep them. The virtue of fortitude helps us have the strength and courage to continue doing the right thing even when it is hard. When we read about Jesus carrying the Cross, we can see that it wasn't easy. Jesus' love for us gave Him the fortitude to keep going despite His pain and sorrow.

◆ Earlier in this Gospel, Jesus asked His followers to take up their cross and follow Him. What do you think that means in your own life?

- What is something that requires you to grow in the virtue of fortitude?
- Who is someone in your life who helps you like Simon of Cyrene?

IT OUT

The Stations of the Cross are a traditional Catholic devotion often prayed during Lent. Originally, pilgrims would travel to the Holy Land and walk the path where Jesus carried the Cross, stopping to pray at the locations of events from Good Friday. Over time, a format for the prayer was created to allow anyone around the world to unite themselves to Jesus in His carrying of the Cross.

Today every Catholic Church and chapel has a set of Stations of the Cross for the faithful to pray with. Fourteen stories from Jesus' Passion and death are highlighted, and while the reflections and prayers can vary, each Station usually begins with the prayer: "We adore You, O Christ, and we praise You, because by Your Holy Cross You have redeemed the world."

If possible, attend one of your parish's Stations of the Cross services this Lent as a family. You also can pray at home using a book or video about the Way of the Cross, or even with your own short reflections. Knowing more about the events of Holy Week will help you fully enter into the joy of Easter.

LECTIO DIVINA

LECTIO
How does this passage describe Jesus' Way of the Cross?

MEDITATIO
Simon of Cyrene helped Jesus carry the Cross. How can we help those who are suffering?

ORATIO
Pray for those who are sick or have chronic pain.

CONTEMPLATIO
Close your eyes and imagine being Simon carrying the Cross with Jesus.

THE Sacred Triduum

After our journey through the desert with Jesus during Lent, we now enter into the Triduum. The Triduum is the shortest liturgical season of the year—only three days! The name for this season comes from those three holy days, which is why it starts with the prefix "tri," just like triangle and tricycle.

Do you know what the three days are? They start at sundown on Holy Thursday when Jesus celebrated the Last Supper, continue through His suffering, death, and burial on Good Friday and Holy Saturday, and end triumphantly when He rises from the dead on Easter Sunday morning.

Holy Week is like a retreat that the whole Church participates in each year. Day by day, we relive the final events of Jesus' life and witness His glorious Resurrection. The special liturgies teach us about the most important aspects of our faith.

As you listen to these stories and spend time in prayer during Holy Week, remember that this is why Jesus came to earth. He did come to teach and serve and heal, but most importantly, He came to die for our sins. It might seem sad, but it's actually the best news ever! Jesus did not stay in the tomb; Good Friday is not the end of the story. We wait for the Easter sunrise and the hope that Jesus brings!

"Holiness consists in one thing: To do God's will, as He wills it, because He wills it."

ST. KATHARINE DREXEL

VISIO DIVINA FOR THE TRIDUUM
Jesus Is Placed in the Tomb *by Albin and Paul Windhausen*

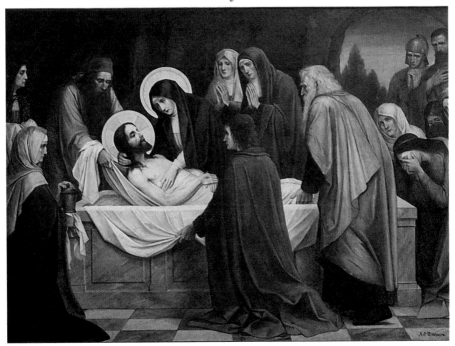

Jesus Is Placed in the Tomb, *Albin and Paul Windhausen, 1914*

Spend some time praying Visio Divina with this painting of the Fourteenth Station of the Cross. Use the same steps as Lectio Divina: *Lectio, Meditatio, Oratio, Contemplatio.* First, slowly examine the art, noticing details and how it tells a story. Then, think about the painting and make connections to what you already know. Finally, take a few minutes to pray about the image, asking God questions as well as listening to what He shares with you.

REFLECTION QUESTIONS

◆ Do you recognize some of the people in this painting? Who might the others be?

◆ What varying emotions do you notice on their faces?

◆ What do you think many of them were thinking as they sealed the tomb and walked away that Good Friday evening?

THE LAST SUPPER
Holy Thursday

LUKE 22:19-20

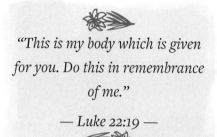

"This is my body which is given for you. Do this in remembrance of me."

— Luke 22:19 —

And he took bread, and when he had given thanks he broke it and gave it to them, saying, "This is my body which is given for you. Do this in remembrance of me." And likewise the chalice after supper, saying, "This chalice which is poured out for you is the new covenant in my blood."

TELL THE *Story*

At the Last Supper on Holy Thursday, Jesus gave us the most wonderful gift. He instituted the Mass and gave us His Body and Blood, which we call the Sacrament of the Eucharist.

The Eucharist is a mystery! The host looks like bread, smells like bread, and tastes like bread, but we believe that the Eucharist is truly Jesus—Body, Blood, Soul, and Divinity. We use a challenging word—Transubstantiation— to define this belief. Remember, it's okay if a mystery is hard to understand. We will learn and study and pray about an important teaching like this our whole lives, but it isn't something that we can ever completely explain or comprehend. Faith helps us to trust that what Jesus says is true.

Jesus gives us His very self in the Sacrament of the Eucharist, so it is important to show great reverence for the Blessed Sacrament. When we are old enough, we can lovingly receive Jesus in Holy Communion. We can show Him the virtue of reverence in the tabernacles of our churches. We can stop and spend a few minutes with Him in Adoration.

The Church says that the Eucharist is both the source and the summit of Christian life. Everything comes from Jesus in the Eucharist and everything leads to Jesus in the Eucharist.

- What similarities do you see in Jesus' words at the Last Supper and the prayers you hear at Mass?
- Why do you think Jesus wanted to give us Himself in the Eucharist?
- What questions do you have about Holy Communion?

LECTIO DIVINA

LECTIO

What did Jesus say about the bread and wine at the Last Supper?

MEDITATIO

Do these words sound familiar? Have you heard them before at Mass?

ORATIO

Pray to Jesus in the Blessed Sacrament and thank Him for remaining with us.

CONTEMPLATIO

Next time you are in church or an Adoration chapel, sit quietly and just listen to Jesus.

Live IT OUT

Along with the gift of the Eucharist, we also see the origin of the Sacrament of Holy Orders at the Last Supper. The apostles followed Jesus' directive to "do this in remembrance of me," and as the first bishops they taught and ordained others to do the same.

As we pray for priests on Holy Thursday, we can ask the intercession of saints who've served the Church throughout the eras, including Venerable Augustus Tolton.

Fr. Tolton's cause for canonization is currently open and he was declared Venerable in 2019. As the first recognized black Catholic priest in the United States, he faced many obstacles to heed the call of his vocation.

Born in Missouri in 1854 into an enslaved family, his father first escaped slavery to fight for the Union in the Civil War and then his mother escaped with her children to freedom across the river in Illinois. Augustus was raised Catholic and had a deep, reverent faith, but he still struggled to be accepted in the town's parishes and Catholic schools. He had an advocate in pastor Fr. Peter McGirr, who recognized Tolton's holiness and encouraged him to follow God's call. When no American seminaries would admit Augustus, he was instead sent to study in Rome and was ordained there in 1886. In Rome, he saw the Universal Church in a new light.

Fr. Tolton was academically gifted, spoke multiple languages, and was a talented musician. After his ordination, he expected to be sent as a missionary to Africa, but was sent back to minister to black Catholics in America. First in his hometown of Quincy, and then in Chicago, good Fr. Gus poured out his life for the people of God. He died at the young age of forty-three but has given us a lasting example of heroic virtue and the power of the Sacrament of Holy Orders.

THE CRUCIFIXION AND DEATH OF JESUS
Good Friday

JOHN 19:17-34

So they took Jesus, and he went out, bearing his own cross, to the place called the place of a skull, which is called in Hebrew Golgotha. There they crucified him, and with him two others, one on either side, and Jesus between them.

Pilate also wrote a title and put it on the cross; it read, "Jesus of Nazareth, the King of the Jews." Many of the Jews read this title, for the place where Jesus was crucified was near the city; and it was written in Hebrew, in Latin, and in Greek. The chief priests of the Jews then said to Pilate, "Do not write, 'The King of the Jews,' but, 'This man said, I am King of the Jews.'" Pilate answered, "What I have written I have written."

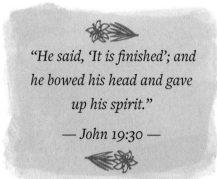

"He said, 'It is finished'; and he bowed his head and gave up his spirit."

— John 19:30 —

When the soldiers had crucified Jesus they took his garments and made four parts, one for each soldier; also his tunic. But the tunic was without seam, woven from top to bottom; so they said to one another, "Let us not tear it, but cast lots for it to see whose it shall be." This was to fulfil the Scripture,

"They parted my garments among them,
and for my clothing they cast lots."

So the soldiers did this. But standing by the cross of Jesus were his mother, and his mother's sister, Mary the wife of Clopas, and Mary Magdalene. When Jesus saw his mother, and the disciple whom he loved standing near, he said to his mother, "Woman, behold, your son!" Then he said to the disciple, "Behold, your mother!" And from that hour the disciple took her to his own home.

After this Jesus, knowing that all was now finished, said (to fulfil the Scripture), "I thirst." A bowl full of vinegar stood there; so they put a sponge full of the vinegar on hyssop and held it to his mouth. When Jesus had received the vinegar, he said, "It is finished"; and he bowed his head and gave up his spirit.

Since it was the day of Preparation, in order to prevent the bodies from remaining on the cross on the sabbath (for that sabbath was a high day), the Jews asked Pilate that their legs might be broken, and that they might be taken away. So the soldiers came and broke the legs of the first, and of the other who had been crucified with him; but when they came to Jesus and saw that he was already dead, they did not break his legs. But one of the soldiers pierced his side with a spear, and at once there came out blood and water.

TELL THE Story

On Good Friday we listen to the story of Jesus' death on the Cross. The Crucifixion is the worst thing that has ever happened, but it is also the best thing that has ever happened. Jesus died to save us from our sins and open the way to Heaven.

When we think about the Crucifixion, it is okay to feel sad about what happened to Jesus. This is a good time to recognize our own sins, ask Jesus for forgiveness, and thank Him for His mercy.

An important event from the Old Testament was fulfilled by the actions of Jesus on Good Friday. In the book of Genesis, Chapter 22, Abraham and Isaac showed us that there would one day be a Lamb of God who would be sacrificed to repair our covenant with God the Father.

You can do an investigation to find all the ways that Jesus and Isaac are connected, especially in the way Jesus died on Good Friday. Both of them were the only beloved son of his father, both carried the wood for the sacrifice on their backs, and both climbed a hill outside Jerusalem. Instead of Isaac, Abraham sacrificed a ram that was caught in thorns, and Jesus, who is called the Lamb of God, was crowned with thorns when He died for us.

- Do you notice any other connections between Jesus and Isaac?
- How did God stop the sacrifice of Isaac?
- An angel was not sent to stop Jesus' Crucifixion, but what happened on Easter morning? Who announced the Resurrection of the Lamb of God?

LECTIO DIVINA

LECTIO

How did Jesus show he loves us on Good Friday?

MEDITATIO

What do you think the Blessed Virgin Mary and St. John were thinking and feeling as they stood at the foot of the Cross?

ORATIO

Pray, "O blood and water, which gushed forth from the heart of Jesus as a fountain of mercy for us, I trust in You."

CONTEMPLATIO

Spend a few minutes of prayer in front of a crucifix today.

Live IT OUT

It is always important to pair the tragedy of Good Friday with the hope of the Resurrection. While our yearly recalling of the events of Holy Week can be hard to talk about, these central tenets of our faith are something that you can discuss with your parents or teacher. Even when remembering Jesus' death on Good Friday, point your eyes toward Him rising from the dead three days later.

THE BURIAL OF JESUS
Holy Saturday

JOHN 19:38-42

After this Joseph of Arimathea, who was a disciple of Jesus, but secretly, for fear of the Jews, asked Pilate that he might take away the body of Jesus, and Pilate gave him leave.

So he came and took away his body. Nicodemus also, who had at first come to him by night, came bringing a mixture of myrrh and aloes, about a hundred pounds' weight. They took the body of Jesus, and bound it in linen cloths with the spices, as is the burial custom of the Jews.

"As the tomb was close at hand, they laid Jesus there."

— John 19:42 —

Now in the place where he was crucified there was a garden, and in the garden a new tomb where no one had ever been laid. So because of the Jewish day of Preparation, as the tomb was close at hand, they laid Jesus there.

TELL THE Story

Today the tabernacles of our churches are empty and there are no Masses or services to attend. The day is quiet and still because we are remembering Jesus lying in the tomb.

We think of the Blessed Virgin Mary, who watched her Son die and be buried. We consider the disciples and the fear and uncertainty they must have felt when Jesus didn't do what they expected. But we also wonder at the work that God did to save us from our sins because we know that Holy Saturday is not the end of the story. We wait in quiet today as the whole world prepares for the power of the Resurrection at sunrise on Easter morning.

The Easter Vigil, a Mass that is held late in the evening of Holy Saturday, breaks the silence of the Triduum. This rich liturgy begins in the dark (like the closed tomb) and moves toward a triumphant celebration of Jesus rising from the dead. If you have the chance to attend as a family, it is a powerful Mass that walks the faithful through salvation history to the mission of Jesus, made complete by the Resurrection.

- Why do you think Holy Saturday is a quiet day?
- What would you think if you were one of the disciples waiting outside the tomb?
- What is hope and why should we think about it on Easter?

IT OUT

To set the tone for Holy Saturday in your home, consider keeping it as a day of "silence" as much as possible. Fast from TV and music to keep your house quiet and make some time for quiet prayer. Contemplate Jesus in the tomb and talk about death and hope as a family. Maybe go for a long walk, pray a Rosary, or stop in for a visit at your church during the day as you prepare your hearts for the celebration of the Resurrection.

There is a beautiful ancient homily that is part of the Office of Readings for Holy Saturday. It is available to read online and captures so well the combined sorrow and hope of this day of waiting during the Triduum. Here are the opening lines:

> What is happening? Today there is a great silence over the earth, a great silence, and stillness, a great silence because the King sleeps; the earth was in terror and was still, because God slept in the flesh and raised up those who were sleeping from the ages. God has died in the flesh, and the underworld has trembled.

LECTIO DIVINA

LECTIO
How did the disciples show their love for Jesus after the Crucifixion?

MEDITATIO
Think about sitting with the Blessed Virgin Mary on this quiet Holy Saturday.

ORATIO
Ask Jesus to fill you with hope for the coming Easter morning.

CONTEMPLATIO
Spend some time in quiet today as if you are waiting at the closed tomb.

THE SEASON OF Easter

Alleluia! He is Risen! He is Risen indeed!

The Resurrection of Jesus Christ is the pinnacle event of our faith. St. Paul wrote in his First Letter to the Corinthians, "If Christ has not been raised, . . . your faith is in vain" (1 Cor 15:14).

Why is the Resurrection such a big deal? When Jesus rose from the dead, He showed us that He is not only fully man but also that He is also fully God. Through His Resurrection, He also gives us hope for eternity. We know that as Christians we follow in Christ's footsteps. Through our Baptism, we are called to die to our old life so that we can rise again with Him, both in the way we live now and in Heaven at the end of our lives.

Easter should be a time of great celebration in your home—and not just on Easter Sunday! After our forty days of fasting, the feasting of the Easter Season lasts for fifty days.

The Octave of Easter stretches over the first eight days of the season, and each day is a Solemnity. A Solemnity is the highest type of liturgical feast, so we can continue to make every day of the Easter Octave a celebration with special food, joyous music, and time in prayer.

The whole Easter Season continues until Pentecost. During the season we hear many stories of the Risen Christ visiting His people and the impact the Resurrection had on the world, even until today. Easter changes everything. As St. Augustine said, "We are an Easter people, and Alleluia is our song!"

"Christ is the morning star who when the night of this world is past brings to his saints the promise of the light of life & opens everlasting day."

ST. BEDE THE VENERABLE

VISIO DIVINA FOR EASTER
The Resurrection of Christ *by Paolo Veronese*

Spend some time praying Visio Divina with this painting of Jesus' Resurrection from the dead. Use the same steps as Lectio Divina: *Lectio, Meditatio, Oratio, Contemplatio.* First, slowly examine the art, noticing details and how it tells a story. Then, think about the painting and make connections to what you already know. Finally, take a few minutes to pray about the image, asking God questions as well as listening to what He shares with you.

The Resurrection of Christ, *Paolo Veronese, 1570*

REFLECTION QUESTIONS

- What do you think the soldiers are feeling at the moment of Christ's Resurrection?
- Notice the pattern of the dark clouds and light in the sky. What do they remind you of?
- What would you think if you were there to witness the first Easter?

THE RESURRECTION

Easter

JOHN 20:1–18

Now on the first day of the week, Mary Magdalene came to the tomb early, while it was still dark, and saw that the stone had been taken away from the tomb. So she ran, and went to Simon Peter and the other disciple, the one whom Jesus loved, and said to them, "They have taken the Lord out of the tomb, and we do not know where they have laid him."

Peter then came out with the other disciple, and they went toward the tomb. They both ran, but the other disciple outran Peter and reached the tomb first; and stooping to look in, he saw the linen cloths lying there, but he did not go in.

Then Simon Peter came, following him, and went into the tomb; he saw the linen cloths lying, and the napkin, which had been on his head, not lying with the linen cloths but rolled up in a place by itself. Then the other disciple, who reached the tomb first, also went in, and he saw and believed; for as yet they did not know the Scripture, that he must rise from the dead.

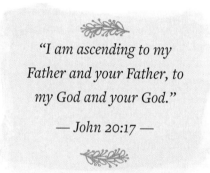

"I am ascending to my Father and your Father, to my God and your God."

— John 20:17 —

Then the disciples went back to their homes.

But Mary stood weeping outside the tomb, and as she wept she stooped to look into the tomb; and she saw two angels in white, sitting where the body of Jesus had lain, one at the head and one at the feet. They said to her, "Woman, why are you weeping?" She said to them, "Because they have taken away my Lord, and I do not know where they have laid him."

Saying this, she turned round and saw Jesus standing, but she did not know that it was Jesus. Jesus said to her, "Woman, why are you weeping? Whom do you seek?"

Supposing him to be the gardener, she said to him, "Sir, if you have carried him away, tell me where you have laid him, and I will take him away."

Jesus said to her, "Mary."

She turned and said to him in Hebrew, "Rab-bo'ni!" (which means Teacher).

Jesus said to her, "Do not hold me, for I have not yet ascended to the Father; but go to my brethren and say to them, I am ascending to my Father and your Father, to my God and your God."

Mary Magdalene went and said to the disciples, "I have seen the Lord"; and she told them that he had said these things to her.

TELL THE *Story*

After the darkness of Jesus' death on Good Friday, Easter Sunday is filled with light. Jesus' enemies thought they had defeated Him, but three days later He rose from the dead! His victory over sin and death reveals to us that He truly is God and that He keeps His promises.

Jesus is alive! He has defeated every obstacle that can keep us from God. Now it is our job to follow the call of our Baptism to die with Christ so that we can rise with Him. To die to ourselves means that instead of only doing what we want with our lives, we listen to God's will and do everything we can to love God and our neighbor.

Jesus loves us enough to not only die for us but also rise for us so that we also can have eternal life. The gift of Easter helps us follow after Him every day with hearts full of joy. Alleluia, He is Risen!

◆ Can you imagine what the disciples were thinking when they saw Jesus alive?
◆ Why do you think Mary Magdalene wasn't able to recognize Jesus right away?
◆ How would you explain Easter to someone else?

Live IT OUT

St. Mary Magdalene is called "the apostle to the apostles" because she was the first to witness the Resurrection and then went to share that good news with Jesus' followers. Her reaction gives us a model to follow in the way we celebrate Easter. First, we should be overjoyed that Jesus overcame the grave and rose from the dead. That joy should then spill over in the ways we love and share the Gospel with others.

Did you know Mary Magdalene is one of the reasons that we use eggs as a symbol of Easter? Many families celebrate Easter Sunday with fun Easter egg hunts, special egg dishes, or egg-shaped candy. The most important reason we use eggs is because an empty eggshell represents the empty tomb after the Resurrection.

There is also a legend that Mary brought cooked eggs to the tomb on Easter morning to share with the other women who came to anoint Jesus. When she discovered that the stone was rolled away and the tomb was empty, she instead ran to tell the apostles. Later when she looked at her eggs, they had miraculously changed from white to red! She used the miracle of the red eggs to tell others about the even more amazing miracle of the Resurrection. Eggs remind us of new life and are ultimately a sign of hope!

LECTIO DIVINA

LECTIO
What did Mary Magdalene do when she found the empty tomb?

MEDITATIO
What would you say if Jesus appeared to you after dying on the Cross?

ORATIO
Pray for those who share the message of Easter with others.

CONTEMPLATIO
Ask Jesus to fill your heart with the wonder of His Resurrection.

JESUS APPEARS TO THOMAS

Divine Mercy

JOHN 20:24-29

> "Put out your hand, and place it in my side; do not be faithless, but believing."
>
> — John 20:27 —

Now Thomas, one of the Twelve, called the Twin, was not with them when Jesus came. So the other disciples told him, "We have seen the Lord." But he said to them, "Unless I see in his hands the print of the nails, and place my finger in the mark of the nails, and place my hand in his side, I will not believe."

Eight days later, his disciples were again in the house, and Thomas was with them. The doors were shut, but Jesus came and stood among them, and said, "Peace be with you." Then he said to Thomas, "Put your finger here, and see my hands; and put out your hand, and place it in my side; do not be faithless, but believing."

Thomas answered him, "My Lord and my God!" Jesus said to him, "You have believed because you have seen me. Blessed are those who have not seen and yet believe."

TELL THE *Story*

Thomas missed out on the first appearance of Jesus to the apostles, and he had a hard time believing what his friends told him. Have you ever heard something that seemed too good to be true? Thomas wanted to see Jesus again, but he also wanted proof of what the others had seen.

One week later Jesus came to the apostles again, and this time Thomas was there! Jesus invited Thomas to touch His hands and His side to see that it really was Him, that He truly had risen from the grave. Thomas responded with a statement of faith, and we can do the same!

This 2nd Sunday of Easter is called Divine Mercy Sunday because it is a perfect reminder of the unending love that Jesus has for all of us.

This event in Thomas' life has earned him the unfortunate nickname of Doubting Thomas. However, we need to remember that this was just part of the bigger story of Thomas' life, a life that resulted in Thomas becoming a saint!

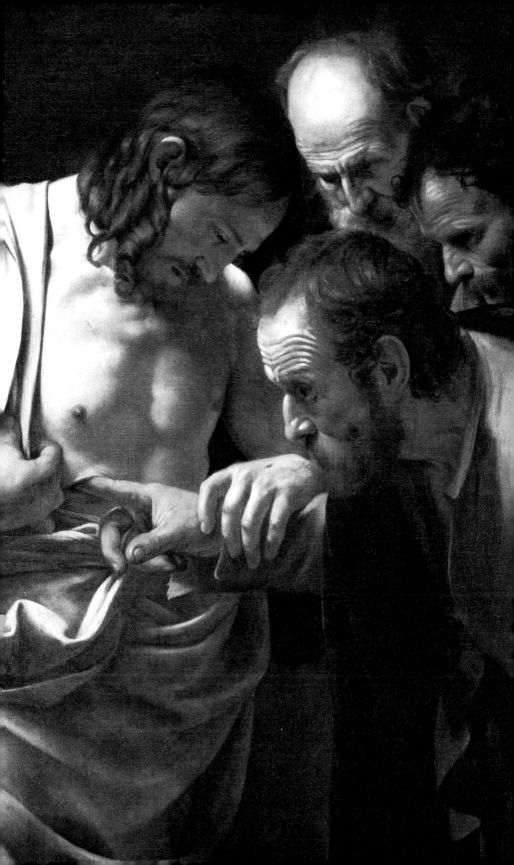

LECTIO
How did Jesus show Thomas that it was really Him?

MEDITATIO
Think about what it would have been like to see Jesus appear even though the doors were locked!

ORATIO
Tell Jesus you will always trust in Him.

CONTEMPLATIO
Do you understand Thomas' doubt and fear? How can you instead choose hope and trust?

Earlier in this same Gospel, Jesus was preparing to go to Jerusalem, where the disciples were beginning to recognize that He would one day suffer and die. In John 11:16, Thomas is the only apostle who says, "Let us also go, that we may die with him."

Archbishop Fulton J. Sheen wrote, "Whatever else may be said of Thomas, it must be admitted that quicker than all the others, he recognized the death that was in store for the Blessed Lord, though he was the last to recognize the Resurrection." Thomas' story is one of hope!

- Have you ever doubted something or someone?
- What did it take for you to believe?
- What can you learn from reading about the mistakes, failures, and doubts of the apostles who then went on to become saints?

Live IT OUT

Divine Mercy Sunday is a wonderful celebration at the end of the Octave of Easter. If you don't have a copy of the Image of Divine Mercy in your home, pull up a picture on your computer. The image is rich in symbolism that all of us can understand. The light in the image is emanating from Christ, showing us that He is the light in the darkness. From Jesus' heart are streams of red and blue light. The red reminds us of His Precious Blood given in the Eucharist and the blue of the waters of Baptism.

You can use the red and blue rays of light as inspiration for your family celebration of Divine Mercy Sunday. Serve pancakes with rows of strawberries and blueberries, hang red and blue streamers, use red and blue watercolors to paint a picture, or have Divine Mercy ice cream sundaes with red and blue sprinkles.

You can also pray the beautiful Divine Mercy Chaplet together or say "Jesus I Trust in You" throughout your day.

VISIO DIVINA FOR EASTER
Landscape with Christ and His Disciples on the Road to
Emmaus *by Jan Wildens*

Landscape with Christ and His Disciples on the Road to Emmaus, *Jan Wildens, 1640s*

Spend some time praying Visio Divina with this painting of the disciples' encounter with Jesus on the road to Emmaus. Use the same steps as Lectio Divina: *Lectio, Meditatio, Oratio, Contemplatio*. First, slowly examine the art, noticing details and how it tells a story. Then, think about the painting and make connections to what you already know. Finally, take a few minutes to pray about the image, asking God questions as well as listening to what He shares with you.

REFLECTION QUESTIONS

- ◆ Imagine walking this road with Jesus and your best friend. What would you talk about? What would you ask Him?
- ◆ Would you want to get to your location quickly and invite Jesus to stay, or would you hope to linger and spend time together on the journey?
- ◆ The artist chose to paint a detailed landscape and sky with Jesus and the two disciples as smaller figures. Why do you think he chose this layout instead of a close portrait of the conversation?

THE ROAD TO EMMAUS
The 3rd Week of Easter

LUKE 24:13-35

That very day two of them were going to a village named Emmaus, about seven miles from Jerusalem, and talking with each other about all these things that had happened. While they were talking and discussing together, Jesus himself drew near and went with them. But their eyes were kept from recognizing him.

And he said to them, "What is this conversation which you are holding with each other as you walk?" And they stood still, looking sad.

Then one of them, named Cleopas, answered him, "Are you the only visitor to Jerusalem who does not know the things that have happened there in these days?"

And he said to them, "What things?" And they said to him, "Concerning Jesus of Nazareth, who was a prophet mighty in deed and word before God and all the people, and how our chief priests and rulers delivered him up to be condemned to death, and crucified him. But we had hoped that he was the one to redeem Israel. Yes, and besides all this, it is now the third day since this happened. Moreover, some women of our company amazed us. They were at the tomb early in the morning and did not find his body; and they came back saying that they had even seen a vision of angels, who said that he was alive. Some of those who were with us went to the tomb, and found it just as the women had said; but him they did not see."

And he said to them, "O foolish men, and slow of heart to believe all that the prophets have spoken! Was it not necessary that the Christ should suffer these things and enter into his glory?" And beginning with Moses and all the prophets, he interpreted to them in all the Scriptures the things concerning himself.

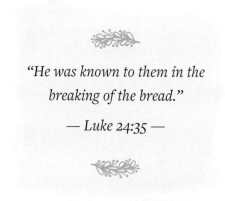

"He was known to them in the breaking of the bread."

— Luke 24:35 —

So they drew near to the village to which they were going. He appeared to be going further, but they constrained him, saying, "Stay with us, for it is toward evening and the day is now far spent." So he went in to stay with them.

When he was at table with them, he took the bread and blessed and broke it, and gave it to them. And their eyes were opened and they recognized him; and he vanished out of their sight.

They said to each other, "Did not our hearts burn within us while he talked to us on the road, while he opened to us the Scriptures?" And they rose that same hour and returned to Jerusalem; and they found the Eleven gathered together and those who were with them, who said, "The Lord has risen indeed, and has appeared to Simon!" Then they told what had happened on the road, and how he was known to them in the breaking of the bread.

TELL THE Story

The Season of Easter is filled with wonderful stories about the Risen Jesus. We often think of Easter as just being about Jesus' Resurrection—which is the most important event of all! But Easter is also about Jesus encountering His people, teaching them, and leading them to act as His disciples as they share the Gospel. Each story during the Easter Season is an invitation for us to encounter Jesus.

Imagine if you were one of the disciples walking with Jesus from Jerusalem to Emmaus. This journey would change your life forever. Jesus not only explained the Scriptures to His disciples, but He also revealed Himself in the breaking of the bread.

Those two actions—teaching from the Bible and breaking the bread—should sound familiar. We do get to "walk to Emmaus" with Jesus every time we participate in Mass! In the Liturgy of the Word, we listen to readings from the Bible and hear our priest teach about what they mean. Then in the Liturgy of the Eucharist, Jesus' Body and Blood are made present through the bread and wine in the Blessed Sacrament.

◆ Do you see any other connections to the Mass in this story?
◆ What do you think the most surprising part of the journey was for the two disciples?
◆ When they rushed back to tell the apostles in Jerusalem, what other news confirmed that Jesus had risen from the dead?

IT OUT

The Road to Emmaus presents a perfect analogy for the Christian experience. Each person's journey toward Christ includes wonder at new information, moments of doubt or misunderstanding, and truth found through prayer and the Sacraments.

Symbolically, the walk from Jerusalem to Emmaus shows us that it is easiest to pursue truth when you are at least moving in the first place. Work to build up a family culture that supports questions, study, and conversations both with one another and with God. Then, just like these disciples after their journey to Emmaus, with burning hearts and open eyes, we can move forward to share the Good News with the whole world.

LECTIO DIVINA

LECTIO
How did the disciples finally recognize Jesus?

MEDITATIO
What do you notice about the way Jesus spoke and interacted with the disciples?

ORATIO
Ask Jesus to help your heart burn within you, especially when you pray at Mass.

CONTEMPLATIO
Think about the words they said to Jesus, "Stay with us."

THE GOOD SHEPHERD
The 4th Week of Easter

JOHN 10:14–18

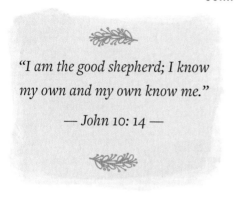

"I am the good shepherd; I know my own and my own know me."

— John 10: 14 —

I am the good shepherd; I know my own and my own know me, as the Father knows me and I know the Father; and I lay down my life for the sheep. And I have other sheep, that are not of this fold; I must bring them also, and they will heed my voice. So there shall be one flock, one shepherd. For this reason the Father loves me, because I lay down my life, that I may take it again. No one takes it from me, but I lay it down of my own accord. I have power to lay it down, and I have power to take it again; this charge I have received from my Father."

TELL THE *Story*

Have you ever met a sheep? They are good animals, but often require lots of protection and help. A shepherd gives his sheep good food and clean water, guides the flock to safe places to rest, and guards his sheep from any danger.

There are many examples of shepherds in the Bible, including King David. Before he became the powerful king of Israel, David was just a shepherd taking care of his flock. He would have learned how to protect and provide for those weaker and smaller than him, and his years in the pastures alone with just the animals surely gave him lots of time to pray and listen to God. David's work as a shepherd made him a better king and also helped him see that God is also like a shepherd.

All of the examples of shepherds in the Old Testament help us to understand why Jesus calls Himself the Good Shepherd. Like a flock of sheep, we need His guidance and protection. Jesus says that His sheep know His voice and follow Him. Most importantly, Jesus acts as our Good Shepherd when He lays down His life and dies to save us.

◆ How does Jesus guide us?
◆ How does Jesus protect us?
◆ How can we listen to Jesus' voice?

LECTIO DIVINA

LECTIO
What title does Jesus give Himself in this story?

MEDITATIO
What would be the difference between a good shepherd and a bad shepherd?

ORATIO
Ask Jesus to help you always listen to His voice.

CONTEMPLATIO
Close your eyes and imagine Jesus as a shepherd guiding and protecting you.

The Fourth Sunday of Easter is celebrated as Good Shepherd Sunday. During the Easter Season, we joyfully look to Jesus as our loving Savior who guides, guards, provides, and protects.

This is also a perfect Sunday to honor our priests and bishops who act as shepherds for our parishes and dioceses. As a family, you can make cards or pray a spiritual bouquet for your pastor and bishop. A spiritual bouquet sounds fancy, but it is simply a collection of prayers for someone's intentions. You can pray any amount and any combination of prayers, but it can be really special to write down the details of the bouquet and send it to the person. Praying for our priests is the greatest gift we can give them!

POWER TO FORGIVE
The 5th Week of Easter

JOHN 20:19–23

On the evening of that day, the first day of the week, the doors being shut where the disciples were, for fear of the Jews, Jesus came and stood among them and said to them, "Peace be with You." When he had said this, he showed them his hands and his side. Then the disciples were glad when they saw the Lord. Jesus said to them again, "Peace be with you. As the Father has sent me, even so I send you." And when he had said this, he breathed on them, and said to them, "Receive the Holy Spirit. If you forgive the sins of any, they are forgiven; if you retain the sins of any, they are retained."

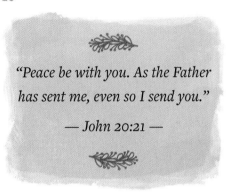

"Peace be with you. As the Father has sent me, even so I send you."

— John 20:21 —

TELL THE Story

After the Resurrection, Jesus gave the apostles everything they needed to lead the new Church. In this story, He first gives them proof that He had risen from the grave! Jesus shows them His hands and His side where there were scars from the Crucifixion. He had been nailed to the Cross and pierced by the lance, but now He was healed!

The disciples rejoiced because they knew He was alive. They also believed in the power of His Resurrected Body because He was able to come into a locked house by appearing and disappearing from their sight. Jesus had performed many miracles during His time on earth, but He certainly showed the disciples even more amazing things after His Resurrection.

After coming to them, Jesus gives them an important message and a job to fulfill. He tells the disciples, the men who became the Church's first bishops, that they could act as ministers of His forgiveness. We recognize now that these instructions were the beginning of the Sacrament of Confession.

Through the work of the Holy Spirit, priests can hear our Confessions and grant us absolution, or forgiveness. But even though they are saying the words of the prayers, it is really Jesus who is forgiving us. We turn to Jesus when we have hurt Him or others, express our sorrow for our sin, and resolve to do it no more. Jesus welcomes us back, forgives us, and gives us His grace to help us go and sin no more.

- How do you feel when you have done something wrong?
- Why is it good to turn to someone and ask for help after you've made a mistake? Do you think that it is amazing that God will forgive our sins?
- What questions do you have about the Sacrament of Confession?

Live IT OUT

The Sacrament of Confession is a true gift from God to His people. If the standard we are held to demanded that we obtain perfection and never sin after first receiving God's grace in our Baptism, we would all fall short. Instead, the Lord provides the tool we need within the Church to not only confess and be forgiven but also be strengthened with His grace as we go forward, allowing us to change and grow and follow His plan for our lives.

If you are old enough to receive the Sacrament of Confession, find an appropriate book or pamphlet to help you prepare well for the Sacrament each time, and plan to receive the Sacrament together as a family. It is a good rule of thumb to go to Confession once per month (unless in a state of mortal sin).

It's okay to feel a little nervous about this Sacrament, but the more it is utilized, the easier it is to see the fruits manifested in our lives. The Sacraments work together as conduits of God's life in the world. Asking for His forgiveness and accepting His absolution is a true gift to the Church.

LECTIO DIVINA

LECTIO
How did Jesus get into the room where the disciples were?

MEDITATIO
In what ways does Jesus show the disciples that He is resurrected both Body and Soul?

ORATIO
Think about ways you've hurt God or others. Ask for Jesus' forgiveness.

CONTEMPLATIO
Pray about the words, "Peace be with you."

JESUS AND PETER AT THE SEA OF TIBERIAS
The 6th Week of Easter

JOHN 21:15–19

When they had finished breakfast, Jesus said to Simon Peter, "Simon, son of John, do you love me more than these?"

He said to him, "Yes, Lord; you know that I love you."

He said to him, "Feed my lambs." A second time he said to him, "Simon, son of John, do you love me?"

He said to him, "Yes, Lord; you know that I love you."

He said to him, "Tend my sheep." He said to him the third time, "Simon, son of John, do you love me?"

Peter was grieved because he said to him the third time, "Do you love me?" And he said to him, "Lord, you know everything; you know that I love you."

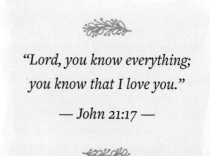

"Lord, you know everything; you know that I love you."

— John 21:17 —

Jesus said to him, "Feed my sheep. Truly, truly, I say to you, when you were young, you fastened your own belt and walked where you would; but when you are old, you will stretch out your hands, and another will fasten your belt for you and carry you where you do not wish to go." (This he said to show by what death he was to glorify God.) And after this he said to him, "Follow me."

TELL THE *Story*

On this early morning following Easter, Peter and some of the disciples had been fishing all night without catching anything. When a man calls to them from the shore, they pull in a miraculous netful of fish! They realize that it is the Risen Jesus because something very similar happened when Jesus first called Peter to be His disciple.

Now Jesus again asks Peter to follow Him. This time, Peter will follow Jesus in order to lead the new Church. Jesus shows him that love will be the key to his ministry.

Why did Jesus ask three times if Peter loved Him? One reason is that during Jesus' Passion and death Peter denied Jesus three times. By asking Peter, "Do you love me?" again and again, Jesus gave him the opportunity

LECTIO DIVINA

LECTIO
What does Jesus ask Peter to do?

MEDITATIO
How do Jesus' instructions help Peter in his new role as the first pope?

ORATIO
Ask God to help you show forgiveness to others, just as He has forgiven you.

CONTEMPLATIO
Quietly tell Jesus how much you love Him.

to repent of his actions and receive forgiveness. Peter may have run away during the Crucifixion, but with God's grace he will now use his boldness and strength to build the Kingdom for Christ.

- This is a story of forgiveness. Have you ever had to ask for forgiveness?
- Have you ever given someone your forgiveness? An act of mercy is so pleasing to the heart of Christ.
- We know that we can forgive others and receive their forgiveness because of the way Jesus first loves and forgives us. How can your family grow in giving and receiving forgiveness?

Live IT OUT

There is no limit on the phrase, "I love you." The love we show to our family, friends, neighbors, and strangers bears repeating over and over. This love is made manifest in both our words and actions.

Another lesson to take away from Jesus and Peter's conversation is the gift of repetition. Just as the sun rises each morning and is still beautiful and powerful, we can demonstrate our love day after day. Making a meal, sharing a hug, singing a favorite song, praying together, or reading a book together at night—these repetitive moments do not have to become mundane. Instead we see that God delights in pattern and continuity and invites us to find joy in declaring our love for one another in both little and big ways day after day.

THE ASCENSION
The 7th Week of Easter

ACTS 1:6–12

So when they had come together, they asked him, "Lord, will you at this time restore the kingdom to Israel?"

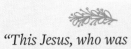

"This Jesus, who was taken up from you into heaven, will come in the same way as you saw him go into heaven."

— Acts 1:11 —

He said to them, "It is not for you to know times or seasons which the Father has fixed by his own authority. But you shall receive power when the Holy Spirit has come upon you; and you shall be my witnesses in Jerusalem and in all Judea and Samaria and to the end of the earth."

And when he had said this, as they were looking on, he was lifted up, and a cloud took him out of their sight. And while they were gazing into heaven as he went, behold, two men stood by them in white robes, and said, "Men of Galilee, why do you stand looking into heaven? This Jesus, who was taken up from you into heaven, will come in the same way as you saw him go into heaven."

Then they returned to Jerusalem from the mount called Olivet, which is near Jerusalem, a sabbath day's journey away.

TELL THE Story

During the Easter Season, we have seen that Easter is not a one-day celebration! Through the stories we hear at Mass and what we have read here together, we rejoice that the Resurrected Jesus spent forty more days with His disciples teaching them, performing miracles, and preparing them for the coming of the Holy Spirit at Pentecost. After those forty days, the time for Jesus to ascend to Heaven had come.

Remember, Jesus is both fully God and fully man. His body ascended into Heaven, but He still remains with us, most especially in the Sacrament of the Eucharist.

Ascension actually falls on a Thursday but is celebrated on the 7th Sunday of Easter in many dioceses. We gather together to listen to Jesus' words to those who gathered near to Him, knowing this message was the last He shared with them during His earthly ministry.

* One of the most important things Jesus told the disciples is that they would be His witnesses. How did the early Christians show the world what they believed about Jesus?
* Where did the disciples go following Jesus' Ascension?
* What were they waiting for there?

Live IT OUT

We were made for Heaven. As we read the story of the Ascension, we see that Jesus' time on earth was always used to direct our lives on earth toward the truth of the eternity of Heaven.

When Jesus ascended, it did not mean that His ministry was over—instead the apostles awaited the coming of the Holy Spirit so that they in turn could go out and continue Jesus' work, which carries forward through the Church today.

To celebrate the Ascension, it can be fun to have a snack or meal with a fluffy white food like whipped cream, marshmallows, or mashed potatoes to remind us of the cloud that lifted Jesus up. Jesus' Resurrection and Ascension is a model of hope intended for each one of us.

LECTIO DIVINA

LECTIO
Where did Jesus say the disciples would be His witnesses? Can you find those places on a map?

MEDITATIO
What would you be thinking if you saw Jesus rise and be taken up by a cloud?

ORATIO
Thank Jesus for His ministry on earth, and for showing us we are made for Heaven.

CONTEMPLATIO
The apostles now had to wait for the coming of the Holy Spirit. Spend some quiet time thinking about how the apostles might have felt, thought, and prayed during the time in between the Ascension and Pentecost.

VISIO DIVINA FOR EASTER
Pentecost *by Jean II Restout*

Pentecost, *Jean II Restout, 1732*

Spend some time praying Visio Divina with this painting of the Holy Spirit's descent at Pentecost. Use the same steps as Lectio Divina: *Lectio, Meditatio, Oratio, Contemplatio*. First, slowly examine the art, noticing details and how it tells a story. Then, think about the painting and make connections to what you already know. Finally, take a few minutes to pray about the image, asking God questions as well as listening to what He shares with you.

REFLECTION QUESTIONS

◆ Where is the source of light in this piece of art? Based on the story of Pentecost, what do you think would be just above the center of the painting?
◆ What symbols of the Holy Spirit do you see throughout the image?
◆ The Blessed Virgin Mary is in the middle of the disciples gathered together to await the coming of the Holy Spirit. What do you notice about her posture and expression compared to the others?

THE DESCENT OF THE HOLY SPIRIT

Pentecost

ACTS 2:1–7

When the day of Pentecost had come, they were all together in one place. And suddenly a sound came from heaven like the rush of a mighty wind, and it filled all the house where they were sitting. And there appeared to them tongues as of fire, distributed and resting on each one of them. And they were all filled with the Holy Spirit and began to speak in other tongues, as the Spirit gave them utterance.

Now there were dwelling in Jerusalem Jews, devout men from every nation under heaven. And at this sound the multitude came together, and they were bewildered, because each one heard them speaking in his own language. And they were amazed and wondered, saying, "Are not all these who are speaking Galileans?"

"And they were all filled with the Holy Spirit."

— Acts 2:4 —

TELL THE Story

Before His Ascension, Jesus told the disciples to wait for the coming of the Holy Spirit in Jerusalem. So, they traveled there and waited together in an upper room. We know that the apostles were in Jerusalem along with the Blessed Virgin Mary, as well as other followers of Jesus. Nine days after Jesus ascended into Heaven, something amazing happened: the Holy Spirit He had promised came!

The Holy Spirit is the third Person of the Blessed Trinity. The Catechism of the Catholic Church paragraph 689 says, "The One whom the Father has sent into our hearts, the Spirit of his Son, is truly God." This Holy Spirit came at Pentecost and works in our lives now through the work of the Church, the Sacraments, and our communication in prayer.

The word "Pentecost" means fiftieth. It was already a traditional Jewish celebration fifty days after Passover but now has deeper meaning for Christians after the coming of the Holy Spirit.

The apostles, gathered together in the upper room, had previously been afraid and uncertain. On the day of Pentecost they boldly went out into Jerusalem telling all who would listen about the Lord Jesus Christ. What's even more amazing is that they shared the Gospel in many, many

languages that they didn't even know how to speak before! Jerusalem was full of visitors for the celebration, and they all heard their message in a way they could understand.

This is a powerful lesson for us. With the help of the Holy Spirit, we never have to be afraid of sharing the Good News of Jesus Christ, and He will always give us the tools we need.

- What would have been the most amazing part of Pentecost to witness?
- Which Gift of the Holy Spirit do you think you could use more of this week?
- What else would you like to discover about the Holy Spirit?

 *Live* IT OUT

A beautiful prayer to pray throughout the day is, "Come, Holy Spirit." While seemingly simple, this invitation into our hearts and homes welcomes the Holy Spirit's power and work in our lives.

The Holy Spirit is present in all Sacraments, but is especially celebrated in the Sacrament of Confirmation. Inviting the Holy Spirit into your home and family prayer can help you prepare your children for receiving Confirmation and living out the graces of the Sacrament.

This Pentecost, welcome the coming of the Holy Spirit with a family celebration filled with His symbols. A few ideas are to have a bonfire (for the tongues of fire that fell on the apostles), color a picture or make a craft of a dove (for the dove that appears in Scripture to represent the Holy Spirit), and make a birthday cake (Pentecost is often called the birthday of the Church).

Learning about the Gifts and the Fruits of the Holy Spirit can also guide your family's discussions about the way the Holy Spirit moves in our lives and helps us form our words and actions to share the mission of the Church, just like the apostles at Pentecost.

LECTIO DIVINA

LECTIO
How is the Holy Spirit described in the Pentecost story? What did the disciples hear, feel, and see?

MEDITATIO
Imagine you were there with Mary and the apostles. What would you think when you heard them speaking about Jesus in all different languages?

ORATIO
Ask the Holy Spirit to fill you with His Gifts of Wisdom, Knowledge, Understanding, Fear of the Lord, Piety, Fortitude, and Counsel.

CONTEMPLATIO
Sit quietly and invite the Holy Spirit to make you brave and ready to share the Gospel.

THE SEASON OF Ordinary Time

Ordinary Time is the only liturgical season that repeats during the year. Actually, we are picking up where we left off in Ordinary Time I, which is why you'll notice the numbering of the weeks doesn't start over. The Church is continuing the journey we started in between the Seasons of Advent and Lent, and this stretch of Ordinary Time II will last all the way until the end of the liturgical year.

Following the end of the Easter Season at Pentecost, we immediately have a few powerful celebrations. The first two Sundays in this part of Ordinary Time are the Solemnity of the Most Holy Trinity and the Solemnity of the Body and Blood of Christ. Nineteen days after Pentecost, the Church celebrates the Solemnity of the Sacred Heart, which always falls on a Friday. Each of these special liturgies reveals more of who Christ is to us: He is part of the everlasting Triune God, He gives us His very self in the Eucharist, and His heart overflows with love and mercy for mankind.

During the remaining twenty or so weeks of Ordinary Time, we will hear stories of Christ's ministry and teaching in the readings at Mass. Over the following chapters, the Gospel stories have been chosen to highlight both Jesus' healing work and miracles as well as some of His most important teachings.

As the end of the liturgical year draws near, the readings at Mass and here in our book turn our gaze toward the time when Christ will come again. We will read about Jesus' judgement and mercy and celebrate His power with the Solemnity of Christ the King on the last Sunday of the year. Ordinary Time is always a time of growth. May we enter into this season with our hearts open and ready to become more like His.

"You pay God a compliment by asking great things of Him."
ST. TERESA OF AVILA

VISIO DIVINA FOR ORDINARY TIME
Stained Glass Window of the Sacred Heart of Jesus

Spend some time praying Visio Divina with this image of the Sacred Heart of Jesus. Use the same steps as Lectio Divina: *Lectio, Meditatio, Oratio, Contemplatio.* First, slowly examine the art, noticing details and how it tells a story. Then, think about the art and make connections to what you already know. Finally, take a few minutes to pray about the image, asking God questions as well as listening to what He shares with you.

Stained Glass Window of the Sacred Heart of Jesus, Cordoba, Spain, Date Unknown

REFLECTION QUESTIONS

◆ Where is Jesus pointing? Can you see any of the symbols on His heart? Do you know their meaning?

◆ We don't have any photographs of Jesus, but He has been depicted countless times in art. When you close your eyes, what do you think Jesus looks like?

◆ This is a photo of a stained glass window. Have you ever noticed the stained glass windows in a church before? The colors being illuminated by light remind us of the beauty that is brought into the world when we allow the light of Christ to shine through us. Take a closer look at the stained glass in the next church you visit.

THE SPIRIT OF TRUTH

The Most Holy Trinity

JOHN 16:12–15

"I have yet many things to say to you, but you cannot bear them now. When the Spirit of truth comes, he will guide you into all the truth; for he will not speak on his own authority, but whatever he hears he will speak, and he will declare to you the things that are to come. He will glorify me, for he will take what is mine and declare it to you. All that the Father has is mine; therefore I said that he will take what is mine and declare it to you."

"When the Spirit of truth comes, he will guide you into all the truth."

— John 16:13 —

TELL THE *Story*

The Holy Trinity is a mystery, but not the type of mystery where a detective looks for clues to solve!

A mystery is a teaching of our faith that is so amazing we can't fit it inside our heads. We can understand parts of a mystery, listen to what the Church teaches, and pray to have deeper truth revealed to us, but we won't fully grasp teachings like the Trinity until we get to Heaven. And that's ok!

God is infinite—all powerful, all knowing, and all present—so it makes sense that we can't fit everything about Him in our heads.

On this Sunday we celebrate the Holy Trinity, God the Father, the Son, and the Holy Spirit. The word "tri" means three, and the Trinity is our belief that there are three Persons in one God. How can this be? The Catholic doctrine (a fancy word for teaching) about the Trinity is considered a mystery.

We know about the Trinity because God has revealed it to us. Remember, it's okay to not understand everything about a mystery, but we can study and read and ask God to help us to know Him more. He shows us the Trinity in the Bible.

♦ Can you think of stories in the Bible about God the Father?
♦ What are some of your favorite stories about Jesus, God the Son?
♦ When do you hear about God the Holy Spirit in the Bible?

LECTIO DIVINA

LECTIO
What does Jesus say the Holy Spirit will bring us?

MEDITATIO
What questions do you have about the passage we just read?

ORATIO
Talk to Jesus about His connection with God the Father and God the Holy Spirit.

CONTEMPLATIO
Think about God the Father, God the Son, and God the Holy Spirit as you slowly make the Sign of the Cross.

Live IT OUT

One way we invoke the Trinity every day is by praying the Sign of the Cross. As we gesture the shape of the Cross over our bodies, remembering that Jesus died to save us, we say the names of the three Persons of the Trinity. Make the Sign of the Cross and say the three names of God within the one prayer.

We also know that we are baptized in the name of the Trinity. As water is poured over us, the minister says, "[*Name*], I baptize you in the name of the Father, and of the Son, and the Holy Spirit." This Trinitarian prayer is the foundation of our faith. Trinity Sunday is a great time to pull out your baptism pictures and talk about the first Sacrament you received!

As you continue to learn more of what has been revealed about the Trinity, it can be fun to use symbols of the Trinity to celebrate what you believe. A triangle, a shamrock, and a Celtic knot are a few common representations. Look around your church. Can you find any symbols of the Trinity embedded in the artwork, stained glass, or architecture?

THE BREAD OF LIFE DISCOURSE
Body and Blood of Christ

JOHN 6:53-58

"He who eats my flesh and drinks my blood abides in me, and I in him."

— John 6:56 —

So Jesus said to them, "Truly, truly, I say to you, unless you eat the flesh of the Son of man and drink his blood, you have no life in you; he who eats my flesh and drinks my blood has eternal life, and I will raise him up at the last day. For my flesh is food indeed and my blood is drink indeed. He who eats my flesh and drinks my blood abides in me, and I in him. As the living Father sent me, and I live because of the Father, so he who eats me will live because of me. This is the bread which came down from heaven, not such as the fathers ate and died; he who eats this bread will live for ever."

TELL THE

St. John Vianney said, "There is nothing so great as the Eucharist. If God had something more precious, He would have given it to us."

Today we read a section of Jesus' teaching about the Eucharist, His Body and Blood, in the Gospel of John Chapter 6. What Jesus was saying seemed to be crazy to some of the people listening—how could He give them His flesh and blood to eat and drink?

Remember that our God is infinitely powerful. He was able to make the whole universe out of nothing, He has existed since before time began, and He knows everything about us . . . even how many hairs are on our head! He is also able to make Himself present in the Eucharist. Under the appearance of ordinary bread and wine and in every Catholic church around the world through all the ages, Jesus comes to us in Holy Communion.

We believe in the Real Presence, meaning that Jesus is truly with us Body, Blood, Soul, and Divinity in the Sacrament. The word for this truth is Transubstantiation. It's okay if this seems too good to be true! Ask Jesus to increase your faith and help you to see Him each time you go to Mass.

Etair ilrrula gaudete cum leticia qui
lem et commi tristicia fuishs ut exultetis
mini fantte et facicmini ab uberibus
omnes qui diligitis cam consolacionis uir. ps.

- Did you know this Sunday is also called the Solemnity of Corpus Christi? This is the Latin name for Body of Christ. *Corpus* means Body and *Christi* means Christ. Now if you hear those words in a prayer or read them, you'll know what they mean!
- Can you think of any other times you've heard a word in a different language at Mass? Did you know what it meant? Next time, ask your parents or teacher and discover them together!

IT OUT

The Friday following Corpus Christi is celebrated as the Solemnity of the Sacred Heart. This feast is a powerful reminder of Jesus' amazing love for His creation.

We see the Sacred Heart depicted in art and statues with Jesus' heart exposed, lit with flames at the top, encircled with the Crown of Thorns, and with the wound in His side. All of these symbols point us to the truth that Jesus loves us so much that He is willing to give us His very self—both through His death on the Cross and in the gift of the Eucharist.

Along with thanking Him for the Sacrament of His Body and Blood, you can also celebrate His Sacred Heart as a family. There are many activities and coloring pages available online to help you learn about the symbolism found in Sacred Heart art, as well as beautiful prayers to the Sacred Heart and delicious Sacred Heart-themed recipes.

LECTIO DIVINA

LECTIO
What does it mean to "abide"? How close does Jesus want us to be to Him?

MEDITATIO
What do you think the disciples thought when they heard Jesus' teaching about the Eucharist? There is more to the story in the rest of John Chapter 6 if you would like to keep reading!

ORATIO
Ask Jesus to increase your faith and belief in His Real Presence.

CONTEMPLATIO
Think about how the Eucharist and Heaven are connected.

THE BEATITUDES

The 11th Week of Ordinary Time

MATTHEW 5:1–12

Seeing the crowds, he went up on the mountain, and when he sat down his disciples came to him. And he opened his mouth and taught them, saying:

"Blessed are the poor in spirit, for theirs is the kingdom of heaven.

"Blessed are those who mourn, for they shall be comforted.

"Blessed are the meek, for they shall inherit the earth.

"Blessed are those who hunger and thirst for righteousness, for they shall be satisfied.

"Blessed are the merciful, for they shall obtain mercy.

"Blessed are the pure in heart, for they shall see God.

"Blessed are the peacemakers, for they shall be called sons of God.

"Blessed are those who are persecuted for righteousness' sake, for theirs is the kingdom of heaven.

"Blessed are you when men revile you and persecute you and utter all kinds of evil against you falsely on my account. Rejoice and be glad, for your reward is great in heaven, for so men persecuted the prophets who were before you."

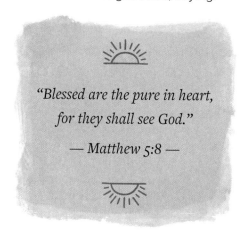

"Blessed are the pure in heart, for they shall see God."

— Matthew 5:8 —

TELL THE Story

What do you think of if you hear a person being described as "blessed"? We might imagine that they have a perfect life with no worries, problems, or conflicts. How does Jesus describe someone who is blessed?

In the Beatitudes, we hear words like "mourn," "poor," and "persecuted," which we wouldn't usually expect to be part of a blessed life.

Jesus wants us to be happy (richly, amazingly, full-to-the-brim joyful!) but we have to remember that our happiness is not dependent on this world. We might experience short-lived happiness from success or pleasure, but that happiness is not made to last. Our true joy will come to fulfillment in Heaven. That is what Jesus is teaching us through the Beatitudes.

We are truly blessed, even when we suffer, as long as we remain united to Him. After listing the characteristics of those who follow Him, Jesus then gives us a promise for how our lives are rewarded by being united to Him. He is showing us how to let go of our attachments to earthly things and instead seek the Kingdom of Heaven.

Jesus is our light and salvation, and whether we are facing good times or challenges, we can always turn to Him to find purpose, peace, and joy.

♦ Which Beatitude's combination of blessing and promise surprises you the most?
♦ Do you have any questions about the meaning of one of the Beatitudes?
♦ Which Beatitude do you think you can work on living out this week?

Live IT OUT

The Beatitudes of the New Testament are often connected to the Ten Commandments in the Old Testament. Both sets of teachings are true and complement rather than contradict one another.

Jesus said that He did not come to abolish the Law, but to fulfill it. Through the Beatitudes, Jesus shows us how to live the Ten Commandments not only with our actions, but also with our hearts. When we look at the details, we see the many parallels between these foundational teachings. Both Moses and Jesus went up a mountain to bring the people the Law, proclaimed it to them, and explained how to live it. Jesus is also the "new" Moses bringing us the Law of the New Covenant. Both were born under the reign of a cruel king, fasted and prayed for forty days in the wilderness, and led their people out of spiritual bondage.

Through the Beatitudes, Jesus shows us once again that the Bible is one unified teaching from beginning to end, calling us to eternal life.

THE BLESSING OF THE CHILDREN
The 12th Week of Ordinary Time

MARK 10:13–16

"Let the children come to me."

— *Mark 10:14* —

And they were bringing children to him, that he might touch them; and the disciples rebuked them. But when Jesus saw it he was indignant, and said to them, "Let the children come to me, do not hinder them; for to such belongs the kingdom of God. Truly, I say to you, whoever does not receive the kingdom of God like a child shall not enter it." And he took them in his arms and blessed them, laying his hands upon them.

TELL THE *Story*

Have you ever felt left out of something because you were too young?

The disciples in this story tried to keep these children from coming close to see Jesus. Maybe they thought He was too busy or the children weren't important enough, but Jesus quickly showed them how much the children mattered.

Jesus loves you, right now, just as you are. He loved you when you were a tiny baby and He'll love you when you are all grown up. You are precious in His sight and He greatly desires that you never be separated from Him. Through our Baptism, we become children of God. He is always our Father, even when we are older.

Just as Jesus blessed the little children in the Gospel, He invites you into a life of blessing for those who trust in Him.

◆ In what ways can you be a child of God even as you grow up?
◆ Where is your favorite place to be close to Jesus?
◆ Can you name some friends who help you follow Jesus?

~~Live~~ IT OUT

God wants us to remain child*like* in our faith. We are called to retain our trust in His goodness, our reliance on His provision, and our acceptance of His will. However, we should not remain child*ish* about what we believe.

Growing, learning, and maturing in our faith is important to every Christian, but that pursuit should not be motivated by pride or control. Instead, our pursuit of Christ should be filled with love. Look to the innocence and wonder of a small child as inspiration for your trust in our Heavenly Father, seeing how He welcomes each of us with open arms.

LECTIO DIVINA

LECTIO
What does Jesus do when the children come near to Him?

MEDITATIO
What questions would you ask Jesus if you were one of the children in this story?

ORATIO
Pray, "Jesus, always keep me close to your heart."

CONTEMPLATIO
Close your eyes and think about Jesus giving you a big hug.

VISIO DIVINA FOR ORDINARY TIME
Let the Little Children Come to Me *by Gebhard Fugel*

Let the Little Children Come to Me, *Gebhard Fugel, 1910*

Spend some time praying Visio Divina with this painting of Jesus welcoming children to Him. Use the same steps as Lectio Divina: *Lectio, Meditatio, Oratio, Contemplatio*. First, slowly examine the art, noticing details and how it tells a story. Then, think about the painting and make connections to what you already know. Finally, take a few minutes to pray about the image, asking God questions as well as listening to what He shares with you.

REFLECTION QUESTIONS

◆ Take a few minutes to examine the expressions on each face. What do you notice?
◆ How does Jesus' posture show that He is welcoming the children?
◆ This painting captures a moment of peace and wonder. What do you think happened next?
◆ What would you ask Jesus if you were one of the children gathered near to Him?

THE LORD'S PRAYER
The 13th Week of Ordinary Time

MATTHEW 6:5–15

"And when you pray, you must not be like the hypocrites; for they love to stand and pray in the synagogues and at the street corners, that they may be seen by men. Truly, I say to you, they have their reward. But when you pray, go into your room and shut the door and pray to your Father who is in secret; and your Father who sees in secret will reward you.

"And in praying do not heap up empty phrases as the Gentiles do; for they think that they will be heard for their many words. Do not be like them, for your Father knows what you need before you ask him. Pray then like this:

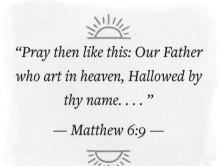

"Pray then like this: Our Father who art in heaven, Hallowed by thy name. . . . "

— Matthew 6:9 —

Our Father who art in heaven,
Hallowed be thy name.
Thy kingdom come.
Thy will be done,
On earth as it is in heaven.
Give us this day our daily bread;
And forgive us our trespasses,
As we forgive those who trespass against us;
And lead us not into temptation,
But deliver us from evil.

"For if you forgive men their trespasses, your heavenly Father also will forgive you; but if you do not forgive men their trespasses, neither will your Father forgive your trespasses."

TELL THE *Story*

Have you ever struggled to find the right words to pray? Prayer is simply a communication of the heart with God, and there are many ways to pray.

In this Gospel passage, Jesus gives the disciples a tool for prayer that has been used by Christians for two thousand years. Within the Our Father, Jesus gives us the perfect combination of praise and petition. We first praise God for who He is and then ask Him for what we need. This order of prayer utilizes the virtue of justice, first giving God everything He deserves and then addressing the needs of our neighbor, and then ourselves.

We can talk to God with our own words, but memorized prayers like the Our Father are important too. They teach us truths about our faith, guide our

communication with God, and give us the words when we aren't sure how to pray. Of all memorized prayers taught by the Church, the Our Father is the most special because it was given to us by Jesus Himself.

- Can you list some of the ways we praise God in the Our Father?
- What are some of the prayers of petition in the Our Father?
- What is one of your favorite memorized prayers? When do you like to pray it?

Live IT OUT

Memorized prayer is truly a gift. In the most difficult moments of our lives when stress and fear and emotion threaten to take over, we can fall back on the treasure of the words of prayer that we know by heart.

We can pray the Prayer for the Faithful Departed when we hear of someone who has passed away, say a Hail Mary for a woman in labor with her baby, or join together in a Glory Be to praise God when we receive good news.

Challenge your family or friends at school to weave Catholic prayers in throughout your day. Learning memorized prayers gives you a toolbox to pull from whenever you need aid—and it will help form your mind and heart.

LECTIO DIVINA

LECTIO
What things does Jesus encourage us to pray for using the Our Father?

MEDITATIO
Why does God not want us to make a big show of our prayers?

ORATIO
Pray the Our Father slowly, thinking about each petition as you pray it.

CONTEMPLATIO
Choose one line from the Our Father to pray quietly about.

PETER'S CONFESSION ABOUT JESUS

The 14th Week of Ordinary Time

MATTHEW 16:13-20

Now when Jesus came into the district of Caesarea Philippi, he asked his disciples, "Who do men say that the Son of man is?"

And they said, "Some say John the Baptist, others say Elijah, and others Jeremiah or one of the prophets."

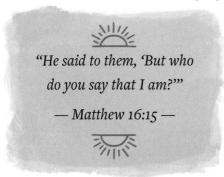

"He said to them, 'But who do you say that I am?'"

— *Matthew 16:15* —

He said to them, "But who do you say that I am?"

Simon Peter replied, "You are the Christ, the Son of the living God."

And Jesus answered him, "Blessed are you, Simon Bar-Jona! For flesh and blood has not revealed this to you, but my Father who is in heaven. And I tell you, you are Peter, and on this rock I will build my Church, and the gates of Hades shall not prevail against it. I will give you the keys of the kingdom of heaven, and whatever you bind on earth shall be bound in heaven, and whatever you loose on earth shall be loosed in heaven."

Then he strictly charged the disciples to tell no one that he was the Christ.

TELL THE Story

St. Peter was bold. Sometimes that boldness caused him to rush and say the wrong thing. But other times Simon Peter was bold and brave in just the right ways.

In this story, Jesus was talking with His disciples about other people's opinions. We believe that Jesus is the Messiah, but He didn't come in the way a lot of people expected. Those who heard about Him thought He might be just another prophet or teacher.

When Jesus asked who people said He was, the apostles listed off those ideas. But when asked "Who do *you* say that I am," Peter boldly proclaimed his faith in Jesus as the Son of God, the Messiah come to save the world.

Because Peter listened, believed, and acted, Jesus revealed that he would become the leader of His Church. He changed his name from

LECTIO DIVINA

✿✿✿

LECTIO

Many people misunderstood who Jesus was. Who were some of their guesses?

MEDITATIO

What do you think Peter's keys are meant to help us remember?

ORATIO

Pray for the pope to be strong as he builds up the Kingdom of God.

CONTEMPLATIO

If someone asked, who would you say Jesus is?

Simon to Peter, which means rock, showing that Peter would be a strong foundation for the spread of the faith. St. Peter became the first pope, and the Catholic Church has been led by an unbroken succession of apostolic leaders from then until now!

◆ What do you think Jesus had in common with John the Baptist, Elijah, Jeremiah, and the prophets?
◆ In what ways do you think you are bold and brave?
◆ How do you share your faith with friends or family members who have different beliefs?

Live IT OUT

Karol Wojtyła faced great obstacles during his lifetime. His mother and older brother both died while Karol was a child, and his father died when he was just twenty. Karol lived in Poland, and during his lifetime it was overtaken by Nazi forces and Communist control. He labored in a rock quarry and a chemical factory, both very dangerous jobs, during the occupation.

But Karol's faith was incredibly strong, leading him to study at an underground seminary and later be ordained a priest. He went on to continue his studies in Rome, pastor several churches in Poland, and become a professor at a seminary. In 1958 he was appointed a bishop, in 1964 an archbishop, and in 1967 a cardinal. And on October 16, 1978, Karol was elected pope. He took the name John Paul II and led the Church as Christ's servant for almost twenty-seven years.

Pope John Paul II traveled and wrote and prayed and inspired the world with his holiness. He is an example for us to follow when we think of how to answer the question, "But who do you say that I am?" St. John Paul II, who is now a saint, showed us with his life that every answer can be found in Jesus.

THE WOMAN AT THE WELL

The 15th Week of Ordinary Time

JOHN 4: 4–15 (OR READ THE WHOLE STORY IN VERSES 4–42)

[Jesus] had to pass through Samaria. So he came to a city of Samaria, called Sychar, near the field that Jacob gave to his son Joseph. Jacob's well was there, and so Jesus, wearied as he was with his journey, sat down beside the well. It was about the sixth hour.

There came a woman of Samaria to draw water. Jesus said to her, "Give me a drink." For his disciples had gone away into the city to buy food.

The Samaritan woman said to him, "How is it that you, a Jew, ask a drink of me, a woman of Samaria?" For Jews have no dealings with Samaritans.

Jesus answered her, "If you knew the gift of God, and who it is that is saying to you, 'Give me a drink,' you would have asked him and he would have given you living water."

The woman said to him, "Sir, you have nothing to draw with, and the well is deep; where do you get that living water? Are you greater than our father Jacob, who gave us the well, and drank from it himself, and his sons, and his cattle?"

Jesus said to her, "Every one who drinks of this water will thirst again, but whoever drinks of the water that I shall give him will never thirst; the water that I shall give him will become in him a spring of water welling up to eternal life."

The woman said to him, "Sir, give me this water, that I may not thirst, nor come here to draw."

"You would have asked him and he would have given you living water."

— John 4:10 —

TELL THE

With modern conveniences like indoor plumbing, it's hard for us to imagine the importance of wells in ancient cultures.

Wells not only served as a shared location to get water for drinking and washing but also as a social hub for community life. Usually the women of the village would come in the early morning or late evening hours to draw water when it was cooler.

Interestingly, this story tells us it was noon when Jesus and the Samaritan woman met. Why was she there at the hottest part of the day? We don't know the woman's whole story, but it seems that she was an outcast. She

was a Samaritan (Jews and Samaritans did not get along), a woman (unmarried men and women didn't interact in public), and a sinner (Jesus was sinless), but her background didn't stop Jesus from talking to her.

Jesus spoke with her, asked her questions, offered her hope, and revealed to her that He was the Messiah. The woman then went and shared her encounter with the whole town, leading many to belief. Jesus shows us that everyone belongs in the Body of Christ!

- ◆ What do you think Jesus meant by living water?
- ◆ Have you ever felt left out? Who in your life makes you feel like you belong?
- ◆ How can you work on being more welcoming to someone who might be different from you?

IT OUT

While she remains unnamed, the woman at the well has similarities with her sisters in the Old Testament. Rebekah, Rachel, and Zipporah all have important stories that take place at wells. Each of them was led to meet her future husband while drawing water at a well.

This pattern makes the well a symbol of marriage, especially one that has God at its center. When you read the whole story of the Woman at the Well, you discover that this woman isn't in a godly marriage. Every New Testament fulfillment surpasses their Old Testament type. Instead of just giving her regular water, Jesus offers her the living water of eternal life. In place of her broken relationship, she is given a community of believers.

The Samaritan woman and her well teach us that Christ desires to reveal Himself to us, give us new life, and then send us out to share the Good News. Practically, she also is a reminder that no one is excluded from God's grace and all are welcome in the Church. Pray this week especially for those who feel separated from Christ or lack community.

LECTIO DIVINA

LECTIO
What did Jesus promise the Samaritan woman?

MEDITATIO
How is water important in our everyday life? How is water used in the Bible and in the Sacraments?

ORATIO
Dear Jesus, help me to always come to You for what I need.

CONTEMPLATIO
Intentionally think about the meaning of Holy Water next time you use it at church.

BLIND BARTIMAEUS
The 16th Week of Ordinary Time

MARK 10:46–52

And they came to Jericho; and as he was leaving Jericho with his disciples and a great multitude, Bartimaeus, a blind beggar, the son of Timaeus, was sitting by the roadside. And when he heard that it was Jesus of Nazareth, he began to cry out and say, "Jesus, Son of David, have mercy on me!" And many rebuked him, telling him to be silent; but he cried out all the more, "Son of David, have mercy on me!"

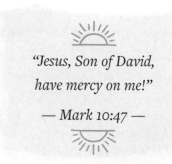

"Jesus, Son of David, have mercy on me!"

— *Mark 10:47* —

And Jesus stopped and said, "Call him."

And they called the blind man, saying to him, "Take heart; rise, he is calling you." And throwing off his cloak he sprang up and came to Jesus.

And Jesus said to him, "What do you want me to do for you?"

And the blind man said to him, "Master, let me receive my sight."

And Jesus said to him, "Go your way; your faith has made you well." And immediately he received his sight and followed him on the way.

TELL THE *Story*

God, the Creator of the universe, is all knowing, but He still wants us to communicate with Him. He sees our needs, but desires us to talk to Him in prayer.

When Jesus asked Bartimaeus what he wanted, Jesus already knew, but He was inviting Bartimaeus to trust and put his faith in God.

Bartimaeus is miraculously healed not by his own power or the strength of his prayers, but because Jesus chose him to receive this gift and share it with the world. When you are praying, ask God for what you want and then have faith that He will give you exactly what you need!

- ◆ The title "Son of David" is another name for the Messiah. The Jews believed that the Messiah would have the ability to heal. What was Bartimaeus proclaiming by calling Jesus the Son of David?
- ◆ What did Bartimaeus do after Jesus healed him?
- ◆ How can we respond to Jesus when something wonderful happens in our life?

LECTIO DIVINA

LECTIO

What did Bartimaeus do when others told him to be quiet?

MEDITATIO

How do you think Bartimaeus knew to ask Jesus for help?

ORATIO

Pray the Jesus Prayer: "Lord Jesus Christ, Son of God, have mercy on me, a sinner."

CONTEMPLATIO

Imagine being blind and then being able to see. What would you say to Jesus?

Live IT OUT

"Take heart; rise, he is calling you." These words from the disciples caused Bartimaeus to jump up and run to Jesus, declaring what he believed and asking for healing.

What if Bartimaeus had listened to the voices that told him to be quiet? Maybe he wouldn't have met Jesus, couldn't have been healed, and, most importantly, might have ignored the opportunity to follow Him.

We all face discouragement. What does discouragement look like in your life? Are there any particular places or people who do not encourage you to be your best self? Take some time to pray this week about how you can listen to voices that lift you up and bring you to Jesus, as well as ways you can be an encouragement to others.

THE PARABLE OF THE LOST SHEEP
The 17th Week of Ordinary Time

MATTHEW 18:10–14

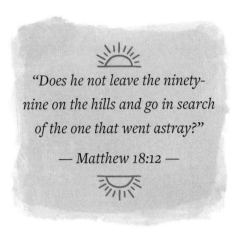

"Does he not leave the ninety-nine on the hills and go in search of the one that went astray?"

— Matthew 18:12 —

"See that you do not despise one of these little ones; for I tell you that in heaven their angels always behold the face of my Father who is in heaven. What do you think? If a man has a hundred sheep, and one of them has gone astray, does he not leave the ninety-nine on the hills and go in search of the one that went astray? And if he finds it, truly, I say to you, he rejoices over it more than over the ninety-nine that never went astray. So it is not the will of my Father who is in heaven that one of these little ones should perish."

TELL THE *Story*

Picture your absolute favorite toy. Now imagine you have one hundred of them! Wouldn't that be amazing? As you are playing with all of these fabulous toys, you realize that one is missing. What would you do? What if while looking for the lost toy, you run the chance of losing the other ninety-nine? Would you do it?

Whether we are talking about toys or sheep, most people would not take a risk with ninety-nine just to gain one more.

However, Jesus our Good Shepherd sees things a little differently. In His flock of sheep, the Church, each one of us is precious, valued, and important. The extreme example in the Parable of the Lost Sheep is meant to grab our attention and help us to understand just how much we matter to God. If we ever stray from Him through the separation of sin, He will stop at nothing to bring us back.

◆ What do you think Jesus' original audience thought about this parable?
◆ What are some ways that we can stray from Jesus like the lost sheep?
◆ How do we know the Good Shepherd welcomes us back to the flock?

Live IT OUT

St. Margaret Mary Alacoque was a French nun who received apparitions of Jesus in the seventeenth century. She is one of the saints who helped spread a devotion to the Sacred Heart.

St. Margaret Mary is an example of the virtue of fidelity, which is repeated faithfulness to what one believes in. Jesus told Sr. Margaret Mary He wanted her to make His love for all people known throughout the world, specifically using the glorious image of His Sacred Heart. Despite many people not believing her, she was obedient to Jesus' message and showed great fidelity in the face of persecution.

The burning love of the Sacred Heart of Jesus and St. Margaret Mary's story both show us that we are never far from God, even when we feel alone.

LECTIO DIVINA

LECTIO
What does the shepherd do when he finds the lost sheep?

MEDITATIO
Why was it surprising that Jesus said a shepherd should leave ninety-nine sheep to find the one lost sheep?

ORATIO
Ask Jesus to help you see those that are lost or alone and help them.

CONTEMPLATIO
What would it be like to be the lost sheep? How would it feel to have God come find you?

THE RAISING OF LAZARUS

The 18th Week of Ordinary Time

JOHN 11:32–44 (OR THE LONGER VERSION IN VERSES 1–44)

Then Mary, when she came where Jesus was and saw him, fell at his feet, saying to him, "Lord, if you had been here, my brother would not have died."

When Jesus saw her weeping, and the Jews who came with her also weeping, he was deeply moved in spirit and troubled; and he said, "Where have you laid him?"

They said to him, "Lord, come and see." Jesus wept. So the Jews said, "See how he loved him!" But some of them said, "Could not he who opened the eyes of the blind man have kept this man from dying?"

> *"'Did I not tell you that if you believed you would see the glory of God?'"*
>
> — John 11:40 —

Then Jesus, deeply moved again, came to the tomb; it was a cave, and a stone lay upon it. Jesus said, "Take away the stone." Martha, the sister of the dead man, said to him, "Lord, by this time there will be an odor, for he has been dead four days."

Jesus said to her, "Did I not tell you that if you would believe you would see the glory of God?" So they took away the stone. And Jesus lifted up his eyes and said, "Father, I thank you that you have heard me. I knew that you always hear me, but I have said this on account of the people standing by, that they may believe that you sent me."

When he had said this, he cried with a loud voice, "Lazarus, come out." The dead man came out, his hands and feet bound with bandages, and his face wrapped with a cloth. Jesus said to them, "Unbind him, and let him go."

TELL THE *Story*

Jesus is a miracle worker. He walked on water and calmed the storm. He made the blind see and the deaf hear. Jesus caused the lame to walk and even cast out demons. The miracles worked by Christ during His ministry were for the individual, but they also impacted the disciples, the crowd, and even the Church today.

Jesus showed His love and care for those that He healed and at the same time taught His people that He truly was the Messiah who had come

LECTIO DIVINA

LECTIO
What does Martha believe about Jesus?

MEDITATIO
Why do you think Jesus wept even though He knew He would raise Lazarus from the dead?

ORATIO
Take a moment to pray for your loved ones who have died.

CONTEMPLATIO
Pretend to be Martha kneeling at Jesus' feet.

with signs and wonders. The story of Lazarus might be the most amazing example because Lazarus had actually died. When Jesus raised His friend from the tomb, He helps us understand that He has power over life and death, not just for Lazarus but for all of us!

* How would this miracle have impacted the crowd gathered at Lazarus' tomb?
* Both Martha and Mary of Bethany were friends and disciples of Jesus. How did they each show faith in Him? (Especially using the whole story in verses 1–44)
* Think about how the raising of Lazarus connects to Jesus' Resurrection. How are they similar? How are they different?

Live IT OUT

Talking about life and death doesn't have to be reserved to just adult conversation. Childlike wonder and the hope of Heaven are a part of our Christian faith and are important to talk about at every age in life.

When you hear about the topic of death, or if you have experienced the death of a loved one, does it bring up any questions inside of you? Read stories from the Bible like the raising of Lazarus, Jesus' Resurrection, and visions of Heaven like those in Revelation 7:15–17 to learn more about what God has told us about life after death. You can also memorize the Prayer for the Faithful Departed and pray it with your family for those who have died.

We were made for eternal life. Everything we do here on earth should point us toward Heaven.

THE PARABLE OF THE MUSTARD SEED

The 19th Week of Ordinary Time

MATTHEW 13:31-32

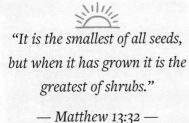

"It is the smallest of all seeds, but when it has grown it is the greatest of shrubs."

— Matthew 13:32 —

Another parable he put before them, saying, "The kingdom of heaven is like a grain of mustard seed which a man took and sowed in his field; it is the smallest of all seeds, but when it has grown it is the greatest of shrubs and becomes a tree, so that the birds of the air come and make nests in its branches."

TELL THE *Story*

Can you name something incredibly tiny? What is that tiny item good for? Does it change over time?

Jesus frequently used everyday objects to teach us spiritual truths. Even if you've never seen a mustard seed, you know that most seeds are fairly small. What is amazing is that each seed has the potential to become a whole plant with roots, stems, leaves, flowers, and fruit. If we looked at the tiny seed and said that it was worthless because it was so small, we'd never receive all of the benefits of what it could become. Jesus looks at us with that same potential and has great plans for our good.

- ◆ Can you think of tiny things that make a big difference in the world?
- ◆ Have you ever watched a plant grow? Isn't it amazing that God packs everything needed to grow a flower or a tree right inside the seed?
- ◆ What are some ways you can see that God has a plan for you?

LIVE IT OUT

Jesus said in Matthew 7:20, "Thus you will know them by their fruits." He was speaking about false prophets being recognized by the result of their words and work.

Just as you know something is an orange tree when it produces oranges and another is an apple tree when it produces apples, we can see the manifestation of our faith through the fruits of our lives.

The Fruits of the Holy Spirit are listed in Galatians 5:22–23 and CCC 1832 and include love, joy, peace, patience, kindness, goodness, generosity, gentleness, faithfulness, modesty, self-control, and chastity. If our soul is the seed in this parable, we can give it the water of grace in the Sacraments, the sunlight of prayer, and the soil of good relationships in the family and Church. As we grow, these fruits are evident, especially when we allow the work of the Holy Spirit to tend, prune, and care for us.

As a family or individually, chose a Fruit of the Holy Spirit to cultivate in your heart and share with the world.

LECTIO DIVINA

LECTIO
What does the tiny mustard seed become?

MEDITATIO
What is something small you can do that makes a big difference?

ORATIO
Praise God that He can do amazing things using even small tools.

CONTEMPLATIO
Imagine the faith inside your heart as a tiny seed. Watch it grow and grow until it becomes a strong tree.

TWO MIRACULOUS HEALINGS
The 20th Week of Ordinary Time

MATTHEW 9:18–26

While he was thus speaking to them, behold, a ruler came in and knelt before him, saying, "My daughter has just died; but come and lay your hand on her, and she will live." And Jesus rose and followed him, with his disciples.

"Take heart, daughter; your faith has made you well."

— Matthew 9:22 —

And behold, a woman who had suffered from a hemorrhage for twelve years came up behind him and touched the fringe of his garment; for she said to herself, "If I only touch his garment, I shall be made well."

Jesus turned, and seeing her he said, "Take heart, daughter; your faith has made you well." And instantly the woman was made well.

And when Jesus came to the ruler's house, and saw the flute players, and the crowd making a tumult, he said, "Depart; for the girl is not dead but sleeping." And they laughed at him. But when the crowd had been put outside, he went in and took her by the hand, and the girl arose. And the report of this went through all that district.

TELL THE *Story*

Have you ever wondered why the woman wanted to touch Jesus' cloak? This connects to a traditional belief that even the tassels on the Messiah's garment had healing powers. It was Jesus Himself who healed her, but He saw evidence of her faith through her interaction with a physical object.

As Catholics, we have many special objects that help us live out our faith. Some of those items are called sacramentals. Not to be confused with the seven Sacraments, a sacramental does not confer grace. Sacramentals include blessings, like making the Sign of the Cross, as well as objects like a crucifix, holy water, relics, rosaries, Stations of the Cross, saint medals, and scapulars. These sacramentals have no power of their own, but present a visual reminder of what we believe. They can act as tools to enhance our daily prayer and practice of the faith for ourselves while also providing an outward witness to others.

LECTIO DIVINA

LECTIO
What did Jesus say to the two people He healed?

MEDITATIO
Why do you think the stories of these two healings are told side by side?

ORATIO
Pray for those you know who are sick in any way to be made well.

CONTEMPLATIO
Imagine reaching out your hand to touch the cloak of Jesus.

◆ Do you have any favorite sacramentals like a rosary or saint medal?
◆ If you could receive a new sacramental, what would it be and why?
◆ Did you know that you can ask your priest to bless your sacramentals? Ask your family if you can take a favorite sacramental and have it blessed after Mass sometime soon!

Live IT OUT

The stories of the Official's Daughter and the Hemorrhaging Woman are interwoven in the Gospel of Matthew, but we aren't specifically told why. Did their families know one another? How had they both heard about Jesus and His healing power? While those details remain unknown, this passage does help us to see the interconnectivity of the Body of Christ.

Jesus came for us all, and when one member of the Body suffers, we all suffer. Jesus did not ignore the woman who touched His cloak in a hurry to get to the official's house. He saw her, loved her, and healed her. His mission is not either/or but is actually about both of them.

A modern-day example of the value of sacrifice can be seen in St. Gianna Beretta Molla. She was a twentieth-century Italian wife, mother, and doctor who lived a life of beautiful holiness as she cared for her patients and young family. During her fourth pregnancy, it was discovered that she had a tumor that put her and the baby's life at risk. She did all she could to protect her child, and her daughter was born well and healthy. Unfortunately, Gianna passed away shortly after. Gianna's family and in particular her fourth child, named Gianna Emanuela, went on to share about the heroic life of their saintly mom and wife.

St. Gianna Molla gives us an example of choosing to follow Christ not only when it is easy, but also when we have to pick up our cross to live like Him.

VISIO DIVINA FOR ORDINARY TIME
The Sermon on the Mount *by Carl Bloch*

The Sermon on the Mount, *Carl Bloch, 1877*

Spend some time praying Visio Divina with this painting of Jesus giving the Sermon on the Mount. Use the same steps as Lectio Divina: *Lectio, Meditatio, Oratio, Contemplatio*. First, slowly examine the art, noticing details and how it tells a story. Then, think about the painting and make connections to what you already know. Finally, take a few minutes to pray about the image, asking God questions as well as listening to what He shares with you.

REFLECTION QUESTIONS

◆ The artist has depicted many different people with various facial expressions and body language. If you were at this event, which person would you want to be?

◆ This painting of the Sermon on the Mount captures one example of a time that Jesus sat down to teach a crowd. Which teaching of Jesus do you imagine listening to while looking at this piece of art?

◆ What colors do you often see Jesus wearing in art? In this painting, He has on a red tunic and is wrapped in a blue mantle. His red and blue clothing is a common combination in classic art and teaches us about Jesus symbolically. The red represents His humanity and the death He would endure to save us. The blue shows us His divinity and reminds us that He is fully God and will welcome us into Heaven. Have you ever noticed Jesus wearing red and blue in paintings or stained glass windows?

THE FEEDING OF THE FIVE THOUSAND

The 21st Week of Ordinary Time

JOHN 6:1–14

After this Jesus went to the other side of the Sea of Galilee, which is the Sea of Tiberias. And a multitude followed him, because they saw the signs which he did on those who were diseased. Jesus went up into the hills, and there sat down with his disciples.

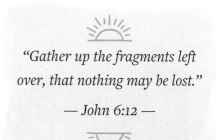

"Gather up the fragments left over, that nothing may be lost."

— John 6:12 —

Now the Passover, the feast of the Jews, was at hand. Lifting up his eyes, then, and seeing that a multitude was coming to him, Jesus said to Philip, "How are we to buy bread, so that these people may eat?" This he said to test him, for he himself knew what he would do. Philip answered him, "Two hundred denarii would not buy enough bread for each of them to get a little."

One of his disciples, Andrew, Simon Peter's brother, said to him, "There is a lad here who has five barley loaves and two fish; but what are they among so many?"

Jesus said, "Make the people sit down." Now there was much grass in the place; so the men sat down, in number about five thousand. Jesus then took the loaves, and when he had given thanks, he distributed them to those who were seated; so also the fish, as much as they wanted. And when they had eaten their fill, he told his disciples, "Gather up the fragments left over, that nothing may be lost." So they gathered them up and filled twelve baskets with fragments from the five barley loaves, left by those who had eaten.

When the people saw the sign which he had done, they said, "This is indeed the prophet who is to come into the world!"

TELL THE *Story*

Have you ever had a big crowd of people at your house for dinner? Maybe it was for a birthday party or to celebrate Christmas. What if you planned for twenty people, but instead fifty people showed up? What if there were one hundred? How about one thousand? It would be crazy to think that the food you had prepared for twenty people would be enough for so many more.

In this amazing miracle, Jesus does just that! A large crowd gathered to listen to Jesus teach, but there wasn't enough food in the area to provide for them. Jesus wanted to show them that He could care for their physical needs so that they would also trust He would provide for their spiritual needs.

During the Exodus of the Israelites from Egypt, God gave His people manna, or bread from heaven, to feed them in the wilderness. Thousands of years later, Jesus multiplied the loaves and the fish, not only to feed their stomachs but also to fill their minds that He is a God of miracles. Later, He'll show them that He is the Bread that has come down from Heaven, which we also receive in the Most Holy Eucharist.

♦ What might have happened if the young boy hadn't been willing to share his loaves and fish?
♦ This story shows us that God can do amazing things using even a small contribution from us. What "loaves and fish" can you offer Jesus?
♦ What connections can you make between the feeding of the five thousand and Jesus' actions at the Last Supper?

IT OUT

Every detail of the Gospel is intentional—even down to the numbers reported in the stories. When Jesus tells the disciples to gather the pieces left over, we should pay attention when we hear that they collected twelve baskets full. That amount shows us the great generosity of God. After feeding more than five thousand people with the equivalent of one family's dinner, there are still leftovers! God will always provide.

Twelve is a holy number that is often repeated in the Bible. It calls to mind the twelve sons of Jacob and the twelve tribes of Israel. Twelve is a symbol of leadership. The twelve tribes of Israel in the Old Testament are fulfilled by the twelve apostles in the New Testament.

Collecting these twelve baskets of miraculous bread is a sign of the work that the apostles will do after Pentecost. They will go out into the world and bring Christ to all the nations, most importantly through the miraculous gift of His Body in the Eucharist under the appearance of bread.

As you read the Bible or listen to the readings at Mass, pay attention to holy numbers which add depth and meaning to the overarching story of Scripture.

LECTIO DIVINA

LECTIO
What small gift helped Jesus feed the five thousand?

MEDITATIO
Why do you think Jesus would make enough food not only to feed the people but also to have so much left over?

ORATIO
Ask Jesus to help you see the small things you can give Him that will bear great fruit in the world.

CONTEMPLATIO
Close your eyes and think about sitting on the hill while Jesus taught.

THE TRANSFIGURATION
The 22nd Week of Ordinary Time

MATTHEW 17:1-8

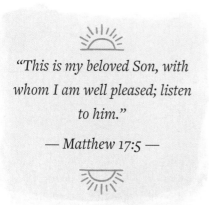

"This is my beloved Son, with whom I am well pleased; listen to him."

— Matthew 17:5 —

And after six days Jesus took with him Peter and James and John his brother, and led them up a high mountain apart. And he was transfigured before them, and his face shone like the sun, and his garments became white as light. And behold, there appeared to them Moses and Elijah, talking with him.

And Peter said to Jesus, "Lord, it is well that we are here; if you wish, I will make three booths here, one for you and one for Moses and one for Elijah."

He was still speaking, when behold, a bright cloud overshadowed them, and a voice from the cloud said, "This is my beloved Son, with whom I am well pleased; listen to him." When the disciples heard this, they fell on their faces, and were filled with awe.

But Jesus came and touched them, saying, "Rise, and have no fear." And when they lifted up their eyes, they saw no one but Jesus only.

TELL THE Story

Have you ever noticed that even though Jesus had thousands of followers and twelve apostles, there are many stories that include only Peter, James, and John? Jesus gave those three men unique opportunities to know Him in a deeper way in order to prepare them for the work they would do after the Resurrection.

Here at the Transfiguration, Peter, James, and John received a little glimpse of Heaven. Jesus was transformed before their eyes and they heard the voice of God the Father.

They also saw Moses and Elijah, both leaders of the faith who had died centuries before. With Moses representing the whole Law and Elijah representing all of the Prophets, Jesus is shown to truly be the fulfillment of the Old Covenant.

The Transfiguration marks an important moment in the lives of Peter, James, and John and helps prepare them to come down from the mountain and share their belief that Jesus truly is the Son of God.

LECTIO

*Who appeared
with Jesus at the
Transfiguration?*

MEDITATIO

*Why do you think
Peter wanted to stay
on the mountain?*

ORATIO

*Thank Jesus for any
special moments
when you have felt
extra close to Him,
like Peter, James,
and John did at the
Transfiguration.*

CONTEMPLATIO

*Pray with the
words, "Rise, and
have no fear."*

♦ Why do you think Peter said, "Lord, it is well that we are here" and asked to stay on the mountain?
♦ What do you know about Moses and Elijah? How is Jesus like them?
♦ Why do you think Jesus spent extra time with Peter, James, and John?

Live IT OUT

The Rosary is like a Bible story on a string. As we say the familiar Our Fathers and Hail Marys, we can meditate on the events of Jesus' life, diving into the details and making connections through prayer.

The Rosary allows us to use our senses— there's the tangible work of moving our fingers to feel the beads and the sound of the prayers we say out loud—and the more mindful work of imagining the Mysteries.

If you've never prayed the Rosary before, don't be afraid to say just one decade at a time. It also can be fun to pick out a rosary that you like. You might find a rosary in your favorite color or with a particular saint medal, or you could even make your own! Little fingers can benefit from bigger, wooden-bead rosaries, and there are even chewy bead rosaries for toddlers and babies!

It can be helpful to have a book or pamphlet with a guide to the prayers to follow along with. You also might want to read short meditations on the Mysteries using the Bible or a Rosary book. You can find more about praying the Rosary on page xx.

Pray the Rosary in the car, at bedtime, or even break up the decades throughout the day.

No matter what, don't give up!

WALKING ON WATER

The 23rd Week of Ordinary Time

MATTHEW 14:22–33

Then he made the disciples get into the boat and go before him to the other side, while he dismissed the crowds. And after he had dismissed the crowds, he went up into the hills by himself to pray.

When evening came, he was there alone, but the boat by this time was many furlongs distant from the land, beaten by the waves; for the wind was against them. And in the fourth watch of the night he came to them, walking on the sea. But when the disciples saw him walking on the sea, they were terrified, saying, "It is a ghost!" And they cried out for fear.

"Take heart, it is I; have no fear."

— *Matthew 14:27* —

But immediately he spoke to them, saying, "Take heart, it is I; have no fear."

And Peter answered him, "Lord, if it is you, bid me come to you on the water."

He said, "Come." So Peter got out of the boat and walked on the water and came to Jesus; but when he saw the wind, he was afraid, and beginning to sink he cried out, "Lord, save me."

Jesus immediately reached out his hand and caught him, saying to him, "O you of little faith, why did you doubt?" And when they got into the boat, the wind ceased. And those in the boat worshiped him, saying, "Truly you are the Son of God."

TELL THE *Story*

Have you ever stood on the shore of an ocean, river, or lake? A large body of water is something incredible to see but it can also be a scary place during a storm.

Many miracles involving water throughout the Bible are evidence of the great power of God. We read in the Old Testament that God controlled the rise of the waters that washed the earth clean while Noah and his family were safe on the ark. He also parted the Red Sea for Moses and the Israelites.

By walking on the stormy sea and then calming the wind and the waves, Jesus showed that He has power over creation. The disciples on the boat

witnessed this miracle and were reassured by Jesus' words: "Take heart, it is I; have no fear." Peter, showing his characteristic combination of eager trust and impulsiveness, climbed out of the boat to come to Christ.

Peter's brave action should inspire us and serve as a reminder to keep our gaze on Jesus, not on the waves and wind around us.

- What would you be thinking if you were in the boat during the storm and saw Jesus walking on water?
- How was Peter brave? How did Peter give in to fear?
- What do you do when you are afraid? How can you keep your eyes on Jesus?

 IT OUT

Coping with fear can be difficult. God does not want us to be afraid, which is made clear by the hundreds of times the Bible includes the words "Have no fear."

A Christian's encounter with fear can be transformed by trust in God and reliance on prayer. Just as every adult should desire to fierce-ly protect a child from any threat, our mighty God is here to defend and save us. While we should always share our fears with our parents, teachers, or a friend, we can also learn to rely on God and the protection of His angels.

Memorizing Scripture like the highlight-ed verse in this passage, as well as praying the St. Michael the Archangel and Guardian Angel Prayers, helps us trust and keep our eyes on Heaven. Prayer is powerful and effective in the face of stress, anxiety, and fear, both over our ex-ternal circumstances and our inner feelings.

LECTIO DIVINA

LECTIO
What caused Peter to sink?

MEDITATIO
How do you think Peter felt when Jesus reached out His hand to save Him?

ORATIO
Ask Jesus to help you have faith when you feel doubt.

CONTEMPLATIO
How might Jesus be asking you to get out of "the boat" and do something brave?

THE PRODIGAL SON

The 24th Week of Ordinary Time

LUKE 15:11-32

"There was a man who had two sons; and the younger of them said to his father, 'Father, give me the share of property that falls to me.' And he divided his living between them. Not many days later, the younger son gathered all he had and took his journey into a far country, and there he squandered his property in loose living. And when he had spent everything, a great famine arose in that country, and he began to be in want. So he went and joined himself to one of the citizens of that country, who sent him into his fields to feed swine. And he would gladly have fed on the pods that the swine ate; and no one gave him anything. But when he came to himself he said, 'How many of my father's hired servants have bread enough and to spare, but I perish here with hunger! I will arise and go to my father, and I will say to him, "Father, I have sinned against heaven and before you; I am no longer worthy to be called your son; treat me as one of your hired servants."'

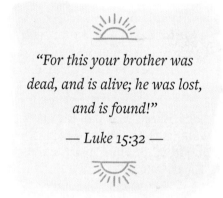

"For this your brother was dead, and is alive; he was lost, and is found!"

— Luke 15:32 —

"And he arose and came to his father. But while he was yet at a distance, his father saw him and had compassion, and ran and embraced him and kissed him. And the son said to him, 'Father, I have sinned against heaven and before you; I am no longer worthy to be called your son.' But the father said to his servants, 'Bring quickly the best robe, and put it on him; and put a ring on his hand, and shoes on his feet; and bring the fatted calf and kill it, and let us eat and make merry; for this my son was dead, and is alive again; he was lost, and is found.' And they began to make merry.

"Now his elder son was in the field; and as he came and drew near to the house, he heard music and dancing. And he called one of the servants and asked what this meant. And he said to him, 'Your brother has come, and your father has killed the fatted calf, because he has received him safe and sound.' But he was angry and refused to go in. His father came out and entreated him, but he answered his father, 'Behold, these many years I have served you, and I never disobeyed your command; yet you never gave me a kid, that I might make merry with my friends. But when this son of yours came, who has devoured

your living with harlots, you killed for him the fatted calf!' And he said to him, 'Son, you are always with me, and all that is mine is yours. It was fitting to make merry and be glad, for this your brother was dead, and is alive; he was lost, and is found.'"

TELL THE  *Story*

One of the most important messages of the story of the Prodigal Son is that we are never too far away from God to come back to Him.

The younger son's actions were cruel and hurtful both to himself and his family. When he realized the depth of his sin, he repented, returned, and was reconciled with his father.

We follow this same pattern when we have hurt God and others with our own sin. We first have to admit our sin and be sorry. Then we go to God, as well as to the people we have hurt, and ask their forgiveness. God then gives us His absolution and we resolve to sin no more.

The Prodigal Son is a perfect reflection to help prepare us to receive the Sacrament of Reconciliation, especially when we look at the father in the story as a model of how God the Father always welcomes us home when we return to Him.

- Have you ever been tempted to run away from a situation, even just to the backyard or your room?
- Did the younger son solve any of his problems by leaving? What do you think helped him be brave enough to come home?
- Did the father behave the way you would expect? What about the older brother? What can we learn from each of these characters?

IT OUT

While usually titled "The Prodigal Son," this parable might be more accurately called "The Merciful Father." Jesus' parables are so effective because all people of every time and place can relate to them.

Our sins are reflected in the actions of both sons, and we cling to the hope of forgiveness that was given by the father. We first learn about mercy in our own homes, so it is important to make sincere apologies and offer true forgiveness when we do something wrong or have been wronged.

What challenges do you face when it comes to apologies and forgiveness?

LECTIO DIVINA

LECTIO
What did the father do when his younger son returned?

MEDITATIO
Why do you think the older brother behaved the way that he did?

ORATIO
Ask God to give you the courage to run to Him when you need His mercy.

CONTEMPLATIO
Imagine God the Father stretching out His arms to welcome you home.

THE HEALING OF A PARALYTIC
The 25th Week of Ordinary Time

LUKE 5:17-26

On one of those days, as he was teaching, there were Pharisees and teachers of the law sitting by, who had come from every village of Galilee and Judea and from Jerusalem; and the power of the Lord was with him to heal. And behold, men were bringing on a bed a man who was paralyzed, and they sought to bring him in and lay him before Jesus; but finding no way to bring him in, because of the crowd, they went up on the roof and let him down with his bed through the tiles into their midst before Jesus.

And when he saw their faith he said, "Man, your sins are forgiven you."

"I say to you, rise, take up your bed and go home."

— Luke 5:24 —

And the scribes and the Pharisees began to question, saying, "Who is this that speaks blasphemies? Who can forgive sins but God only?"

When Jesus perceived their questionings, he answered them, "Why do you question in your hearts? Which is easier, to say, 'Your sins are forgiven you,' or to say, 'Rise and walk'? But that you may know that the Son of man has authority on earth to forgive sins"—he said to the man who was paralyzed—"I say to you, rise, take up your bed and go home."

And immediately he rose before them, and took up that on which he lay, and went home, glorifying God.

And amazement seized them all, and they glorified God and were filled with awe, saying, "We have seen strange things today."

TELL THE Story

During His earthly ministry, sometimes the sick approached Jesus and other times their friends and family brought them to Jesus for healing.

When we need healing, whether in mind, body, or soul, we can always go straight to Jesus. We can talk to Him in prayer. We can draw close to Him while reading the Bible. We can encounter Him in the Sacraments.

But it is also wonderful to have our friends and family bring us close to Jesus, too. They might pray in intercession for us or invite us to church when we are struggling. You can do the same. Never hesitate to pray for

LECTIO DIVINA

LECTIO

How did the people know Jesus had healed the paralytic's body? How did Jesus demonstrate the healing of the paralytic's soul?

MEDITATIO

Why do you think Jesus performed miracles like healing the paralyzed man?

ORATIO

Lord, open our eyes to see all of the ways you perform both little and big miracles in our lives.

CONTEMPLATIO

Close your eyes and think about the gift Christ gave to the paralyzed man by forgiving his sins and restoring his mobility. Then quietly ponder the gifts He has given you.

someone who is sick, sad, afraid, or alone. Be the kind of friend who tells them that they are loved not only by you, but also by God Himself.

◆ How would you describe the friends that brought this man to Jesus?
◆ What does it mean to be a good friend? Are you a good friend to your siblings and classmates?
◆ Do you have good friends in your life? What do you appreciate about them?

Live IT OUT

Jesus' healing ministry was not reserved to His time walking the earth. The Church continues His good work for the sick and dying through the Sacrament of Anointing of the Sick.

The Sacrament is not reserved only for those near death. A person can also receive Anointing of the Sick when facing a long-term illness or an upcoming surgery. When possible, it is often received alongside the Sacraments of Confession and the Eucharist, giving the person who is ill every grace possible.

We always pray for a complete healing of the body if it be God's will, but understand that the spiritual effects of Anointing of the Sick also include a union of our suffering with Christ's Passion, strength and courage to face illness, forgiveness of sins, and preparation for eternal life.

You can read more about Anointing of the Sick in James 5:14–15 and Mark 6:12–13 as well as in the Catechism of the Catholic Church, paragraphs 1499–1532.

ASK, SEEK, KNOCK

The 26th Week of Ordinary Time

MATTHEW 7:7–11

"Ask, and it will be given you; seek, and you will find; knock, and it will be opened to you. For every one who asks receives, and he who seeks finds, and to him who knocks it will be opened. Or what man of you, if his son asks him for bread, will give him a stone? Or if he asks for a fish, will give him a serpent? If you then, who are evil, know how to give good gifts to your children, how much more will your Father who is in heaven give good things to those who ask him!"

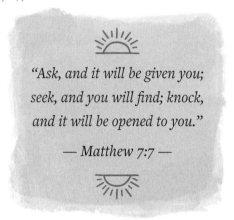

"Ask, and it will be given you; seek, and you will find; knock, and it will be opened to you."

— *Matthew 7:7* —

TELL THE *Story*

Close your eyes and think of some of the blessings in your life. What are they?

God desires to give you good things. Some of those good gifts will be in this life, and many of them will be in Heaven. When Jesus instructs us to ask, seek, and knock, He is showing us that we can always come to Him in prayer. We can ask Him for blessings for ourselves and others, but every prayer should always be connected to the will of God.

Jesus told us that we will receive and find and have the door opened to us. However, this doesn't mean that we can pray and have something we want magically fall from the sky. Jesus is much more amazing and powerful than a wish-granting genie from a fairy tale, and we need to be careful to not just list off the things we want in prayer.

When you pray in your own words, use a balance of praising God, telling Him you are sorry, thanking Him, and also asking for the things you need. Talking to Jesus in all of these ways helps us align our prayer to His will.

◆ What is something you can ask Jesus in prayer today?
◆ How do you try to seek God's will when you make decisions?
◆ How might Jesus be "knocking" on your heart? In what ways can you better listen to Him?

Live IT OUT

One of the greatest struggles of faith we can encounter is the seemingly unanswered prayer. How can we understand the response of God, especially when it is different than we would expect?

We are called to ask, seek, and knock as this passage instructs, but then to wait, trust, and hope in God's will.

Archbishop Fulton J. Sheen shared this wisdom: "You cannot always depend on prayers to be answered the way you want them answered but you can always depend on God. God, the loving Father often denies us those things which in the end would prove harmful to us. Every boy wants a revolver at age four, and no father yet has ever granted that request. Why should we think God is less wise? Someday we will thank God not only for what He gave us, but also for that which He refused."

A practical pattern to guide prayer is the acronym "ACTS." You can use these steps out loud, during silent prayer, or when journaling.

A stands for Adoration and helps us start our prayer in a rightly ordered way by praising God for who He is.

C stands for Contrition, which reminds us to examine our consciences, express sorrow for our sin, and resolve to do better.

T stands for Thanksgiving. Here we thank God for the many blessings we have been given.

S stands for Supplication, which is where we bring our needs and the needs of others before God.

LECTIO DIVINA

LECTIO
How does Jesus describe His generosity in this teaching?

MEDITATIO
What are some of the ways God has answered your prayers?

ORATIO
Tell Jesus how grateful you are for His love and provision in your life.

CONTEMPLATIO
Spend some time thinking about how you can respond to other people with generosity.

THE GREATEST COMMANDMENT
The 27th Week of Ordinary Time

MARK 12:28–34

And one of the scribes came up and heard them disputing with one another, and seeing that he answered them well, asked him, "Which commandment is the first of all?"

Jesus answered, "The first is, 'Hear, O Israel: The Lord our God, the Lord is one; and you shall love the Lord your God with all your heart, and with all your soul, and with all your mind, and with all your strength.' The second is this, 'You shall love your neighbor as yourself.' There is no other commandment greater than these."

And the scribe said to him, "You are right, Teacher; you have truly said that he is one, and there is no other but he; and to love him with all the heart, and with all the understanding, and with all the strength, and to love one's neighbor as oneself, is much more than all whole burnt offerings and sacrifices."

And when Jesus saw that he answered wisely, he said to him, "You are not far from the kingdom of God." And after that no one dared to ask him any question.

"You shall love the Lord your God with all your heart, and with all your soul, and with all your mind, and with all your strength."

— *Mark 12:30* —

TELL THE

Which commandment do you think is the most important?

It would be hard enough to narrow down the Ten Commandments given to Moses—it is possible the scholars were debating a much bigger list! Traditionally, there were six-hundred-and-thirteen laws or commandments contained throughout the Old Testament.

Jesus reveals the wisdom of the plan of God by summarizing them into two categories, either relating to love of God or love of neighbor. If you think about it, all of the rules that you follow at home and school should follow this pattern too.

◆ What rules do you have at home or school that help you love God with your heart, soul, mind, and strength?

LECTIO DIVINA

LECTIO
What does Jesus say is the greatest commandment?

MEDITATIO
What do you think it means to love God with all your strength?

ORATIO
Lord, show me how I can love You above all things. Lead me to love my neighbor as myself.

CONTEMPLATIO
Think about the words heart, soul, mind, and strength related to how we love God.

◆ What rules do you have at home or school that help you love your neighbor as yourself?
◆ Beyond rules, how can you work on loving God and your neighbor more? Remember, your "neighbor" could be anyone—your sibling, classmate, or even a person on the other side of the world!

Live IT OUT

The Greatest Commandment recited by Jesus has its origin in the Shema prayer, which is found in Deuteronomy 6:4–9. The Shema was important to the Jewish people in the time of Jesus and still is today. The fullness of the Law is contained within this Greatest Commandment.

When we examine the Ten Commandments, the first three primarily relate to our love of God and the last seven correspond to our love of neighbor. By teaching these two commandments in the Gospels, Jesus is upholding everything taught in the Old Testament. But He also draws our eyes to focus on the theme of love that is both the source and purpose behind the Law we have been given.

When making a decision, ask, "How does this help me love God?" followed by, "How does this help me love my neighbor?"

VISIO DIVINA FOR ORDINARY TIME
Christ's Entry into Jerusalem *by Jean-Hippolyte Flandrin*

Christ's Entry Into Jerusalem, *Jean-Hippolyte Flandrin, 1846*

Spend some time praying Visio Divina with this painting of Jesus entering into Jerusalem. Use the same steps as Lectio Divina: *Lectio, Meditatio, Oratio, Contemplatio*. First, slowly examine the art, noticing details and how it tells a story. Then, think about the painting and make connections to what you already know. Finally, take a few minutes to pray about the image, asking God questions as well as listening to what He shares with you.

REFLECTION QUESTIONS

- Have you ever been to a big parade? How did the people in the crowd act? What did they focus on? What similarities and differences do you see in this crowd as Jesus enters Jerusalem?
- We see many expressions of worship in this painting. Can you find someone with their head bowed? Someone with their hands folded and another with their hands open? People standing, kneeling, and bowed low to the ground? What is your favorite posture for prayer?
- Many of the people are holding palm branches. These palms represent the victory and triumph of a kingdom as well as the peace of eternal life. The crowd welcomed Jesus as their King! What symbols do we use in our homes and churches to show Jesus is the King of Heaven and earth?

THE ENTRY INTO JERUSALEM
The 28th Week of Ordinary Time

MARK 11:1–11

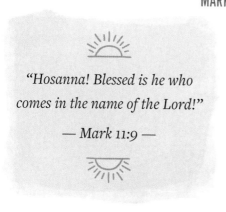

"*Hosanna! Blessed is he who comes in the name of the Lord!*"

— *Mark 11:9* —

And when they drew near to Jerusalem, to Bethphage and Bethany, at the Mount of Olives, he sent two of his disciples, and said to them, "Go into the village opposite you, and immediately as you enter it you will find a colt tied, on which no one has ever sat; untie it and bring it. If any one says to you, 'Why are you doing this?' say, 'The Lord has need of it and will send it back here immediately.'"

And they went away, and found a colt tied at the door out in the open street; and they untied it. And those who stood there said to them, "What are you doing, untying the colt?" And they told them what Jesus had said; and they let them go. And they brought the colt to Jesus, and threw their garments on it; and he sat upon it. And many spread their garments on the road, and others spread leafy branches which they had cut from the fields. And those who went before and those who followed cried out,

"Hosanna! Blessed is he who comes in the name of the Lord! Blessed is the kingdom of our father David that is coming! Hosanna in the highest!"

And he entered Jerusalem, and went into the temple; and when he had looked round at everything, as it was already late, he went out to Bethany with the Twelve.

TELL THE *Story*

We most often think about Jesus' entry into Jerusalem on Palm Sunday at the beginning of Holy Week in the spring, so it might seem funny to read this story near the end of the liturgical year. However, this was one earthly event where Jesus was celebrated and welcomed as a king.

The palms, the praise, and the parade of people were all foretold in the Old Testament. The prophets even wrote that He would humbly ride on a colt. In Jerusalem, the people threw their cloaks on the ground for Him to ride on, almost as if they were laying down their lives for him. They cut palm branches to wave and spread on the ground, each an act of worship and triumph seen in the Old Testament. And they cried out, "Hosanna!" a prayer

LECTIO DIVINA

LECTIO
How do the people show honor to Jesus as He enters Jerusalem?

MEDITATIO
What do you think it would be like to be among the crowd on that first Palm Sunday?

ORATIO
Pray, "Hosanna! Blessed is he who comes in the name of the Lord!"

CONTEMPLATIO
Quietly think about welcoming Jesus as the King of your heart.

asking to be saved, which turned into a shout of praise for He who had come to save them. Jesus, whose name means "God saves," had indeed come to redeem them and rule over them.

As the liturgical year comes to a close, we read and think about Christ the King and His rule over Heaven and earth.

- If Jesus rode into our city now, what would people lay before Him or wave above Him to show their love, praise, and worship?
- Jesus' name means "God saves" and Christ means "Anointed One." Do you know the meaning of any other names or titles of Jesus?
- What are some of your favorite songs that help you praise Jesus?

Live IT OUT

Among the many types and styles of prayer, we sometimes forget singing is prayer too!

The people's shout when Jesus entered Jerusalem lifted their voices in unified praise. When we sing, we join the words of our prayers with the movement of our whole body in singing.

There are many different types of Christ-centered music that can expand and deepen our prayer. From hymns sung at Mass to songs we hear on a Christian radio station, the lyrics of these songs can help us memorize Scripture, introduce new words to use in prayer, and give us an outward expression of joy and comfort.

The Psalms themselves were written to be sung, so you can find recordings of the Responsorial Psalms to listen to or whole songs inspired by the verses. It also is meaningful to explore Gregorian chant, instrumental sacred music, hymns, or musical adaptations of prayers like the Divine Mercy Chaplet to aid times of prayer. The gift of music can help us to "Sing to the LORD, bless his name; tell of his salvation from day to day" (Ps 96:2).

THE ANOINTING AT BETHANY

The 29th Week of Ordinary Time

MARK 14:3–9

And while he was at Bethany in the house of Simon the leper, as he sat at table, a woman came with an alabaster jar of ointment of pure nard, very costly, and she broke the jar and poured it over his head.

But there were some who said to themselves indignantly, "Why was the ointment thus wasted? For this ointment might have been sold for more than three hundred denarii, and given to the poor." And they reproached her.

But Jesus said, "Let her alone; why do you trouble her? She has done a beautiful thing to me. For you always have the poor with you, and whenever you will, you can do good to them; but you will not always have me. She has done what she could; she has anointed my body beforehand for burying. And truly, I say to you, wherever the gospel is preached in the whole world, what she has done will be told in memory of her."

"Wherever the gospel is preached in the whole world, what she has done will be told in memory of her."

— Mark 14:9 —

TELL THE *Story*

While she remains anonymous in this passage, in the Gospel of John the woman who anoints Jesus is named as Mary of Bethany, the sister of Lazarus. Mary was a disciple and friend of Jesus. She had listened to His teaching and witnessed the miracle when He raised her brother from the dead. Then she brought a jar of expensive oil to anoint Jesus while He was with a group of people in Bethany.

Anointing is an act that declares something set apart for God. For example, an altar that will be used in the Holy Sacrifice of the Mass is anointed before use, and holy objects set apart for the temple were anointed during the time of the Old Testament. Israel's kings were anointed, as are we during the Sacraments of Baptism, Confirmation, Holy Orders, and Anointing of the Sick. Mary's generous and extravagant anointing of Jesus was a public act of worship near the time of His death.

- What are some extravagant ways someone has shown that they love you?
- How have you shown extravagant love for others?
- Some of the people in this story disagreed with how Mary of Bethany used the oil. What do you think gave her the courage to follow through with her plan?

 IT OUT

After this anointing, Jesus said that Mary would be remembered wherever the Gospel is told. This promise was carried out through the inclusion of the anointing at Bethany in the writings of the New Testament.

Jesus, and the Bible as a whole, presents unique stories of women believers. Common society at the time treated women as second-class citizens in many ways, but Jesus did the opposite. Women were counted among His followers. He spoke with them and taught them. Women were at the foot of the Cross and then were first to the tomb on Easter morning. Even Jesus' genealogy in the Gospel of Matthew unusually includes five women—Tamar, Rahab, Ruth, Bathsheba, and the Blessed Virgin Mary.

Jesus and, by extension, the Church uphold the dignity of women and invite them to use their gifts to change the world.

LECTIO DIVINA

LECTIO
Why were some of the people upset with the woman's actions? How did Jesus respond?

MEDITATIO
What stories would you want told by people who remember you?

ORATIO
Pray, "Jesus, help me use my time, talent, and treasure to show honor and love to You."

CONTEMPLATIO
Think about having a disposition of reverence toward God and holy things.

THE PARABLE OF THE WEDDING FEAST

The 30th Week of Ordinary Time

MATTHEW 22:1–14

And again Jesus spoke to them in parables, saying, "The kingdom of heaven may be compared to a king who gave a marriage feast for his son, and sent his servants to call those who were invited to the marriage feast; but they would not come. Again he sent other servants, saying, 'Tell those who are invited, Behold, I have made ready my dinner, my oxen and my fat calves are killed, and everything is ready; come to the marriage feast.'

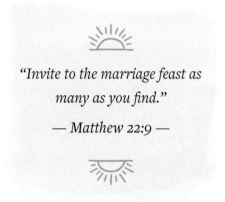

"Invite to the marriage feast as many as you find."

— Matthew 22:9 —

"But they made light of it and went off, one to his farm, another to his business, while the rest seized his servants, treated them shamefully, and killed them. The king was angry, and he sent his troops and destroyed those murderers and burned their city.

"Then he said to his servants, 'The wedding is ready, but those invited were not worthy. Go therefore to the streets, and invite to the marriage feast as many as you find.' And those servants went out into the streets and gathered all whom they found, both bad and good; so the wedding hall was filled with guests.

"But when the king came in to look at the guests, he saw there a man who had no wedding garment; and he said to him, 'Friend how did you get in here without a wedding garment?' And he was speechless. Then the king said to the attendants, 'Bind him hand and foot, and cast him into the outer darkness, where there will be weeping and gnashing of teeth.' For many are called, but few are chosen."

TELL THE *Story*

What do you think Heaven will be like? There are many glimpses of Heaven we can catch in the Bible, but the comparison to a wedding is found all throughout Scripture.

Jesus is called the Bridegroom and the Church is called the Bride of Christ. Now, this can be hard to imagine! We have an earthly understanding of marriage being between one man and one woman, but the comparison of Heaven and a wedding is a parable. Jesus frequently used objects and situations we could all relate to in order to help us grasp a heavenly mystery.

This story of the Wedding Feast is a strong reminder that we are all called to eternity in Heaven, but we must accept the invitation.

◆ We receive our heavenly wedding garment through the grace of our Baptism. How do we keep our "wedding garment" ready throughout the rest of our lives? (Hint: we were given the gift of another Sacrament to help.)
◆ What other symbols or descriptions of Heaven have you heard of?
◆ What do you think we can do to help others accept Jesus' invitation to know and love Him?

Live IT OUT

While we can't describe the details of Heaven with certainty, we do know that Heaven will be a place of infinite love. St. Josephine Bakhita understood this and the gift that comes from accepting the King's invitation to the Eternal Wedding Banquet. She said, "I am definitively loved and whatever happens to me I am awaited by this love."

You might think that Josephine's faith was simple, but her story is one of profound forgiveness, conversion, and hope.

Born in Sudan around 1869, she was kidnapped as a child and sold into slavery. Beaten so badly by the slave traders that she forgot her past and even her own name, they called her Bakhita, which mockingly meant "lucky." She was later sold to an Italian consul, taken to Italy, and resold as a caretaker of a young girl.

Accompanying the girl to a school run by Canossian Sisters, Bakhita learned about Jesus and her identity as a beloved child of God. She was baptized in 1890 and chose to take the new name of Josephine.

When the family decided to return to Africa, Josephine refused to leave the Sisters. Slavery had actually been illegal in Italy since 1895, so with the Sisters' help, Josephine won the legal freedom that she had deserved all along. She took vows and joined the Canossians shortly after.

Josephine's life was marked with peace and she expressed her deep forgiveness to those who had hurt her. St. Josephine Bakhita was canonized in 2000 and is a beacon of light for the world to know that all are welcome to accept the invitation to the Kingdom of Heaven.

LECTIO DIVINA

LECTIO

What did the invited guests do that was wrong? What could they have chosen to do instead?

MEDITATIO

The man without the wedding garment wasn't prepared and didn't take the king's invitation seriously. What are some ways that we can be careless in how we treat prayer, the Sacraments, or Jesus Himself?

ORATIO

Ask Jesus to give you clarity in always following His will.

CONTEMPLATIO

Ponder the idea that God has chosen you to be His own.

WASHING THE FEET OF THE DISCIPLES

The 31st Week of Ordinary Time

JOHN 13:1–15

Now before the feast of the Passover, when Jesus knew that his hour had come to depart out of this world to the Father, having loved his own who were in the world, he loved them to the end.

And during supper, when the devil had already put it into the heart of Judas Iscariot, Simon's son, to betray him, Jesus, knowing that the Father had given all things into his hands, and that he had come from God and was going to God, rose from supper, laid aside his garments, and tied a towel around himself. Then he poured water into a basin, and began to wash the disciples' feet, and to wipe them with the towel that was tied around him.

He came to Simon Peter; and Peter said to him, "Lord, do you wash my feet?"

Jesus answered him, "What I am doing you do not know now, but afterward you will understand."

Peter said to him, "You shall never wash my feet."

Jesus answered him, "If I do not wash you, you have no part in me."

Simon Peter said to him, "Lord, not my feet only but also my hands and my head!"

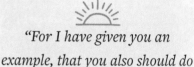

"For I have given you an example, that you also should do as I have done to you."

— John 13:15 —

Jesus said to him, "He who has bathed does not need to wash, except for his feet, but he is clean all over; and you are clean, but not all of you." For he knew who was to betray him; that was why he said, "You are not all clean."

When he had washed their feet, and taken his garments, and resumed his place, he said to them, "Do you know what I have done to you? You call me Teacher and Lord; and you are right, for so I am. If I then, your Lord and Teacher, have washed your feet, you also ought to wash one another's feet. For I have given you an example, that you also should do as I have done to you."

TELL THE *Story*

During the Last Supper, Jesus did something totally unexpected. He washed the apostles' feet! Now this seems quite unusual to us today, but it was even more surprising back then.

LECTIO DIVINA

LECTIO
What example did Jesus give the apostles?

MEDITATIO
How can we live out His call to "wash one another's feet"?

ORATIO
Pray, "Dear Jesus, just as you care for me and show me mercy, give me the strength to be a servant to my family and friends."

CONTEMPLATIO
Close your eyes and imagine Jesus washing your feet before the Last Supper.

With no cars, buses, or trains in the time of Jesus, people's main transportation was their own two feet. Combine sandals and dusty roads over many miles, and you end up with dirty, stinky feet.

The job of taking off a guest's sandals and washing their feet before a meal was usually saved for a household servant. But here, at this last meal with His friends, Jesus redefined the role of a servant. By washing their feet Himself, He showed that a Christlike leader does not desire power for his own sake, but instead uses that power to tend to the needs of others.

Jesus is a Servant-King, and He invites us to follow His example.

◆ How do your parents demonstrate servant leadership to you and your siblings?
◆ What other adults do you have in your life who model Christlike leadership? Grandparents, Godparents, teachers, or coaches?
◆ How can you show this kind of love, especially to others less "powerful" than you?

Live IT OUT

At Holy Thursday Mass each Triduum, before the Memorial of the Lord's gift of the Eucharist, the celebrant takes off his outer vestments and washes the feet of his parishioners. This act of humility modeled directly after Christ is both moving to watch and humbling to receive.

Not every member of a parish can be chosen during that liturgy, but there is no reason a family cannot wash one another's feet at home. By taking turns and allowing everyone in the family, big and little, the chance to care for another in this meaningful way, the ministry of Jesus continues within our domestic churches. "If I then, your Lord and Teacher, have washed your feet, you also ought to wash one another's feet."

THE VINE AND THE BRANCHES
The 32nd Week of Ordinary Time

JOHN 15:1–10

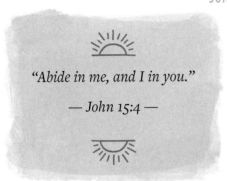

"Abide in me, and I in you."

— *John 15:4* —

"I am the true vine, and my Father is the vinedresser. Every branch of mine that bears no fruit, he takes away, and every branch that does bear fruit he prunes, that it may bear more fruit. You are already made clean by the word which I have spoken to you. Abide in me, and I in you. As the branch cannot bear fruit by itself, unless it abides in the vine, neither can you, unless you abide in me. I am the vine, you are the branches. He who abides in me, and I in him, he it is that bears much fruit, for apart from me you can do nothing. If a man does not abide in me, he is cast forth as a branch and withers; and the branches are gathered, thrown into the fire and burned. If you abide in me, and my words abide in you, ask whatever you will, and it shall be done for you. By this my Father is glorified, that you bear much fruit, and so prove to be my disciples. As the Father has loved me, so have I loved you; abide in my love. If you keep my commandments, you will abide in my love, just as I have kept my Father's commandments and abide in his love."

TELL THE *Story*

Do you have a favorite team sport to watch or play?

Basketball, volleyball, hockey, softball . . . all of them require unity among the players as they work together toward their goal. If one player is following Plan A while another is using Plan B, the whole team will suffer.

Jesus' Parable of the Vine and the Branches has many similarities. God the Vinedresser is like the coach who sets the mission and gives the players what they need. The branches can't get their job done alone. If they separate themselves from the vine, they are like the player who refuses to cooperate with their teammates and listen to their coach.

But Jesus wants us to thrive and succeed. We do that by remaining in Him, part of God's team, and connected to the source of all that is good. The virtue of gratitude also helps us to thank God for the many gifts He has given us, including the people in our lives who help us to grow.

- Can you think of a time you couldn't get along with a teammate, sibling, or friend? Were you able to accomplish anything good together during that time?
- Who is someone that has helped you to grow? How are you grateful for them?
- If you were to write your own parable about God being a coach, what would it be like?

 IT OUT

To abide means to dwell or have a home in.

When Jesus instructs us to abide in Him as He abides in us, external circumstances like location don't matter. Remaining in Him has more to do with our openness to prayer and the effort we make to stay connected.

That internal work within our soul is easier when we allow time and space to encounter God away from the busyness and noise of the world. It can be worthwhile to periodically evaluate our homes and schedules, asking if there are built-in opportunities for prayer, locations conducive to our spiritual needs, and opportunities for receiving the Sacraments of the Eucharist and Confession.

With thought and effort, we can remain firmly connected to the Vine and the nourishment that comes from the Vinedresser.

LECTIO DIVINA

LECTIO
What do you think it means for a Christian to bear fruit?

MEDITATIO
To abide means to dwell in a place of rest and love. How can you abide with God?

ORATIO
What makes somewhere feel like home? How can we connect those feelings to our forever home in Heaven?

CONTEMPLATIO
Think about the words, "Abide in me, and I in you."

THE JUDGEMENT OF THE NATIONS
The 33rd Week of Ordinary Time

MATTHEW 25:31–46

"When the Son of man comes in all his glory, and all the angels with him, then he will sit on his glorious throne. Before him will be gathered all the nations, and he will separate them one from another as a shepherd separates the sheep from the goats, and he will place the sheep at his right hand, but the goats at the left.

"Then the King will say to those at his right hand, 'Come, O blessed of my Father, inherit the kingdom prepared for you from the foundation of the world; for I was hungry and you gave me food, I was thirsty and you gave me drink, I was a stranger and you welcomed me, I was naked and you clothed me, I was sick and you visited me, I was in prison and you came to me.'

"Then the righteous will answer him, 'Lord, when did we see you hungry and feed you, or thirsty and give you drink? And when did we see you a stranger and welcome you, or naked and clothe you? And when did we see you sick or in prison and visit you?'

"And the King will answer them, 'Truly, I say to you, as you did it to one of the least of these my brethren, you did it to me.'

"Then he will say to those at his left hand, 'Depart from me, you cursed, into the eternal fire prepared for the devil and his angels; for I was hungry and you gave me no food, I was thirsty and you gave me no drink, I was a stranger and you did not welcome me, naked and you did not clothe me, sick and in prison and you did not visit me.'

"Then they also will answer, 'Lord, when did we see you hungry or thirsty or a stranger or naked or sick or in prison, and did not minister to you?' Then he will answer them, 'Truly, I say to you, as you did it not to one of the least of these, you did it not to me.' And they will go away into eternal punishment, but the righteous into eternal life."

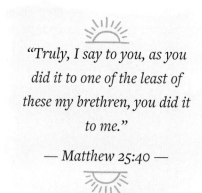

"Truly, I say to you, as you did it to one of the least of these my brethren, you did it to me."

— Matthew 25:40 —

TELL THE *Story*

The motto of St. Benedict, *"Ora et Labora,"* means pray and work. Prayer is essential to the life of a Christian, but it also must be paired with holy work.

One of the most important ways to do God's work is by caring for His people. We can feed and clothe them, visit and care for them. Jesus asks us to be His hands and feet here on earth. He can minister through your actions, and your actions are also ministering to Him. This mystery is true because everyone is a member of the Body of Christ.

The vision of Heaven in this Scripture passage shows us just how much our prayer and work matter.

- What are some ways you can help feed the hungry?
- How can you visit the sick or welcome the stranger?
- Which of these acts of mercy would you like to put into practice in your home? In your school? In your community?

IT OUT

The Church uses this passage to form the list of the Corporal Works of Mercy (while also including burying the dead). All of these deal with caring for the needs of a person's body.

The Church also gives us the Spiritual Works of Mercy to care for the needs of the soul. The Spiritual Works of Mercy are to instruct the ignorant, counsel the doubtful, comfort the afflicted, admonish the sinner, bear wrongs patiently, forgive offenses, and pray for the living and the dead.

While these are important works, they don't need to wait for a specific service trip or until we are adults. All of the Works of Mercy begin primarily in family life and can certainly be lived out by children. Pouring a cup of milk for a younger sibling, accepting an apology with kindness, and helping fold laundry all fit within Jesus' call.

If we are sensitive to the needs of our community and world, it is important that we also find ways to live out the Works of Mercy in a wider sense. We are all called to listen to Jesus' words that when we minister to our least brothers and sisters, we are actually serving Him.

LECTIO DIVINA

LECTIO
What actions had the sheep done to show their love for God's people?

MEDITATIO
Why do you think they were surprised that their actions were really for Jesus?

ORATIO
Pray about the words "You did it to me," thinking about how your acts of service to your family and friends are a way to show love to Jesus.

CONTEMPLATIO
Sit quietly and think about the wonder of Christ the King on His throne in Heaven.

THE COMING OF THE SON OF MAN
Christ the King

MARK 13:24–31

"Heaven and earth will pass away, but my words will not pass away."

— *Mark 13:31* —

"But in those days, after that tribulation, the sun will be darkened, and the moon will not give its light, and the stars will be falling from heaven, and the powers in the heavens will be shaken. And then they will see the Son of man coming in clouds with great power and glory. And then he will send out the angels, and gather his elect from the four winds, from the ends of the earth to the ends of heaven.

"From the fig tree learn its lesson: as soon as its branch becomes tender and puts forth its leaves, you know that summer is near. So also, when you see these things taking place, you know that he is near, at the very gates. Truly, I say to you, this generation will not pass away before all these things take place. Heaven and earth will pass away, but my words will not pass away."

TELL THE Story

Jesus Christ is King of Heaven and earth!

Our Lord created the whole world from nothing at the beginning of time. He came to us as a tiny baby, grew, taught, fed, healed, died for our sins, and rose from the grave. Jesus will come again at the end of time to usher in a New Heaven and a New Earth.

The Bible tells us about this future event, and we do not need to be afraid. We simply place our trust in Jesus as we continue to fulfill the mission He places before us each day.

◆ What is your favorite story about a miracle Jesus performed?
◆ What is your favorite lesson or parable Jesus taught?
◆ Which event from Jesus' life would you most like to have witnessed?

LECTIO DIVINA

LECTIO
What are some of the signs in nature that are described in this passage?

MEDITATIO
What do you think Jesus means when He says He will gather the people from the four winds and the ends of the earth?

ORATIO
Pray, "O Lord, help me to never fear the future but to trust you with each day of my life."

CONTEMPLATIO
Spend a few minutes imagining the glory of Heaven.

 IT OUT

Scripture tells us that the whole world could not contain the books if everything about Jesus were written down.

So much of what we wonder about and hope for will be discovered in Heaven. Here on earth, we will face trials, but Jesus Christ has overcome the world and never wants us to fear the future. Sr. Faustina Maria Pia of the Sisters of Life wrote a beautiful prayer called the Litany of Trust (available online) that is a wonderful tool to pray with as we walk toward eternity.

VISIO DIVINA FOR ORDINARY TIME
The Disputation of the Blessed Sacrament *by Raphael*

The Disputation of the Blessed Sacrament, *Raphael, 1510*

Spend some time praying Visio Divina with this painting of both Heaven and earth. Use the same steps as Lectio Divina: *Lectio, Meditatio, Oratio, Contemplatio*. First, slowly examine the art, noticing details and how it tells a story. Then, think about the painting and make connections to what you already know. Finally, take a few minutes to pray about the image, asking God questions as well as listening to what He shares with you.

REFLECTION QUESTIONS

♦ This amazing painting features a great number of figures, including saints, apostles, popes, artists, scholars, and angels. First, can you find God the Father, Jesus, and the Holy Spirit? Near Jesus, can you see the Blessed Virgin Mary and St. John the Baptist?

♦ Do you see any other people you know based on their symbols? Can you find St. Peter holding keys and St. Paul holding a sword? Where is Moses with the Ten Commandments and David with a crown and a harp?

♦ Below Jesus' throne, angels are holding open four books. What do you think they represent? Can you think of four very important books in the Bible?

◆ This huge fresco (which is about sixteen feet tall and twenty-five feet wide!) is painted in the Apostolic Palace at the Vatican in Rome. Our eye is drawn to the center, where we see the Persons of the Trinity, but also a monstrance on an altar. Through art, we are reminded that the Church is united in Heaven and on earth through the gift of the Most Holy Eucharist. Jesus Christ, King of the Universe, is fully present Body, Blood, Soul, and Divinity in the Blessed Sacrament. How does this painting make you think differently about the connection between the Mass and Heaven?

AFTERWORD

We've come to the end of the liturgical year. So, now what?

Like a beautiful spiral rising up toward Heaven, we begin again! This book is intended to be used as a repeatable resource or a tool to reference in the future.

We are created to read, study, and pray with the stories of Christ over and over, not with a one-and-done mentality. Revisiting the same stories at a later time will certainly not yield the same conversations after a year or two has passed, especially as we grow and learn. Revisiting the Gospel again and again encourages us to see the depth of Jesus' love for us, and each time we read it, we may discover a new and personal message that God has for our lives.

To utilize this book again during another liturgical year, here are a few suggestions:

◆ Practically speaking, it is likely that some of the weekly readings or certain elements of a page weren't used the first time through. On a second reading, revisit alternate questions or go deeper with one of the connecting ideas.

◆ Try using the Lectio Divina prompts or conversation starters as tools for journaling. Instead of just talking about it out loud, slow down and write down reflections and prayers.

◆ Look up the connecting stories from parallel Gospels, and then compare and contrast the details.

◆ You also can use the reflections about the Mysteries of the Rosary while praying the decades.

◆ Following the model of the Lectio Divina prayer starters, read and pray with other stories in the Gospel not included in the ones chosen for the book.

◆ You can also prepare for the Gospel that will be read at the upcoming Sunday Mass by using Lectio Divina and setting aside time for conversation and prayer.

As the Catechism of the Catholic Church says, "In the sacred books, the Father who is in heaven comes lovingly to meet his children, and talks with them" (CCC 104). May we all see Sacred Scripture, especially the Gospels, as an invitation to a lifelong encounter with the God of the Universe.

ACKNOWLEDGEMENTS

JMJ

"We always thank God, the Father of our Lord Jesus Christ, when we pray for you, because we have heard of your faith in Christ Jesus and of the love which you have for all the saints, because of the hope laid up for you in heaven. Of this you have heard before in the word of the truth, the gospel."

— Colossians 1:3–5 —

In profound gratitude:
To the entire team at Emmaus Road Publishing, especially Melissa Girard, for your vision, guidance, advocacy, and hard work that helped bring this practical tool into homes and classrooms.

To Steph, Steven, Emily, Luke, Danielle, Mia, Bonnie, Kayla, Lindsay, and Betsy for the meaningful feedback and practical ideas that made this book so much better, as well as for your encouragement and support during the entire writing adventure.

To Kewanee Vicariate RENEW Group, especially Barb Liska. You were the first ones to encourage me to share my catechetical ideas through a blog and workshops. Praise God for the good work done over all the years since then!

To the pastors, staff, students, and families at Immaculate Conception Catholic Church in Lacon, IL, St. Philomena Catholic Church and School in Peoria, IL, and St. Joseph Catholic Church and School in Pekin, IL. This book is a fruit of the many conversations, classes, Bible studies, and liturgies we have shared together.

To *Look to Him and Be Radiant* readers. I never cease to be amazed by the community that has been created through our sharing of resources for teaching about Christ and His Church. Please know that you, your students, and your families are included daily in my prayers.

To the good and holy priests who have formed, taught, and ministered to me, bringing the Gospel to life through your words and actions. May the Sacred Heart of Jesus bless you abundantly.

To God be all the Glory!

ATTRIBUTIONS

Page 2: Fra Angelico | *The Annunciation* | 1430 | Convent of San Marco, Florence, Italy

Page 4: Masolino da Panicale | *The Annunciation* | c. 1423 | National Gallery of Art, Washington, D.C.

Page 7: Raphael | *Visitation* | 1517 | Museo del Prado, Madrid, Spain

Page 10: Daniele Crespi | *Joseph's Dream* | c. 1620–1630 | Kunsthistorisches Museum, Vienna, Austria

Page 13: Raphael | *Madonna of Loreto* | 1509 | Condé Museum, Chantilly, France

Page 16: Federico Barocci | *The Nativity* | 1597 | Museo del Prado, Madrid, Spain

Page 18: Guido Reni | *The Adoration of the Shepherds* | c. 1640 | National Gallery, London, England

Page 21: Peter Paul Rubens | *The Adoration of the Magi* | c. 1619 | Royal Museums of Fine Arts Belgium, Brussels, Belgium

Page 24: Francesco Trevisani | *The Baptism of Christ* | 1723 | Leeds Art Gallery, Leeds, England

Page 26: Pietro Perugino | *The Baptism of Christ* | c. 1498 | Kunsthistorisches Museum, Vienna, Austria

Page 29: Jean Bourdichon | *The Presentation in the Temple* | c. 1499 | J. Paul Getty Museum, Los Angeles, California

Page 32: Raffaello Sanzio | *The Holy Family with a Lamb* | 1507 | Museo del Prado, Madrid, Spain

Page 35: Ludovico Mazzolino | *The Twelve-Year-Old Jesus Teaching in the Temple* | 1524 | Gemäldegalerie, Berlin, Germany

Page 38: Artist unknown | *God the Geometer* | c. 1250 | Austrian National Library, Vienna, Austria

Page 40: Jacopo Tintoretto | *The Wedding Feast of Cana* | 1545 | Isabella Stewart Gardner Museum, Boston, Massachusetts

Page 42: Artist unknown | c. 1608–1613 | Chiesa di Santa Maria a Novoli, Florence, Italy

Page 46: Federico Barocci | *The Calling of Saints Peter and Andrew* | c. 1590–1609 | Palace Museum in Wilanów, Warsaw, Poland

Page 49: Diego Velázquez | *The Crucifixion* | 1632 | Museo del Prado, Madrid, Spain

Page 51: Michael Pacher | *The Threefold Temptation of Christ* | 1481 | St. Wolfgang Church, St. Wolfgang im Salzkammergut, Austria

Page 55: Titian | *St. John the Baptist* | c. 1550 | Museo del Prado, Madrid, Spain

Page 58: Martin Johann Schmidt | *Christus am Ölberg* | c. 1800s | Private Collection

Page 62: Giovanni Domenico Tiepolo | *The Flagellation of Christ* | c. 1700s | Location unknown

Page 65: Jacopo Tintoretto | *The Flagellation of Christ* | c. 1587–1592 | Capitoline Museums, Rome, Italy

Page 68: Raphael | *Christ Falling on the Way to Calvary* | c. 1516 | Museo del Prado, Madrid, Spain

Page 71: Albin and Paul Windhausen | *Jesus Is Placed in the Tomb* | 1914 | Basilica of Saint Nicholas, Amsterdam, Netherlands

Page 73: Peter Paul Rubens | *Last Supper* | c. 1632 | Pinacoteca di Brera, Milan, Italy

Page 77: Sebastiano Mazzoni | *Raising of the Cross* | c. 1660 | Private Collection

Page 80: Raphael | *The Deposition* | 1507 | Galleria Borghese, Rome, Italy

Page 83: Paolo Verones | The Resurrection of Christ | 1570 | Gemäldegalerie, Dresden, Germany

Page 85: Guadenzi Ferrari | *Christ Rising From the Tomb* | c. 1530–1546 | National Gallery of Art, Washington, D.C.

Page 89: Caravaggio | *The Incredulity of Saint Thomas* | c. 1602 | Sanssouci Picture Gallery, Potsdam, Germany

Page 91: Jan Wildens | *Landscape with Christ and His Disciples on the Road to Emmaus* | c. 1640 | Hermitage Museum, Saint Petersburg, Russia

Page 93: Bartolomeo Cavarozzi | *The Supper at Emmaus* | c. 1615–1625 | J. Paul Getty Museum, Los Angeles, California

Page 97: Bartolome Esteban Murillo | *Christ the Good Shepherd* | c. 1660 | Museo del Prado, Madrid, Spain

Page 100: Jean Auguste Dominique Ingres | *Jesus Returning the Keys to St. Peter* | 1820 | Musée Ingres, Montauban, France

Page 103: Peter Paul Rubens | *Christ's Charge to Peter* | c. 1616 | The Wallace Collection, London, England

Page 106: Pietro Perugino | *The Ascension* | c. 1495–1498 | Museum of Fine Arts of Lyon, Lyon, France

Page 108: Jean II Restout | *Pentecost* | 1732 | Louvre Museum, Paris, France

Page 110: Juan Bautista Mayno | *Pentecost* | c. 1615–1620 | Museo del Prado, Madrid, Spain

Page 113: Artist unknown | Stained Glass Window of the Sacred Heart of Jesus | Date unknown | Cordoba, Spain

Page 115: Jusepe de Ribera | *The Trinity* | c. 1635 | Museo del Prado, Madrid, Spain

Page 118: Limbourg Brothers | *Trés Riches Heures du duc de Berry* | c. 1411–1416 | Condé Museum, Chantilly, France

Page 121: Jan Brueghel the Elder | *The Sermon on the Mount* | 1598 | J. Paul Getty Museum, Los Angeles, California

Page 124: Benjamin Haydon | *Christ Blessing the Little Children* | 1837 | Walker Art Gallery, Liverpool, England

Page 126: Gebhard Fugel | *Lasset die Kindlein zu mir kommen* | 1910 | Museum Abtei Liesborn, Wadersloh, Germany

Page 128: Artist unknown | *Jesus Christ* | 1700 | St. Sophia's Cathedral, Kiev, Ukraine

Page 131: El Greco | *Saint Peter in Tears* | c. 1587–1596 | El Greco Museum, Toledo, Spain

Page 134: Josef von Hempel | *Christus und die Samariterin am Brunnen* | 1823 | Location unknown

Page 137: Workshop of Fernando Gallego | *The Healing of the Blind Bartimaeus* | c. 1480–1488 | University of Arizona Museum of Art, Tucson, Arizona

Page 140: Joseph Ritter von Fürich | *The Good Shepherd* | c. 1840 | Museum Kunstpalast, Düsseldorf, Germany

Page 143: Rembrandt Harmenszoon van Rijn | *The Raising of Lazarus* | c. 1630–1632 | Los Angeles County Museum of Art, Los Angeles, California

Page 146: Jan Luyken | *Etching of the Parable of the Mustard Seed from the Bowyer's Bible* | Date unknown | Location unknown

Page 149: Paolo Veronese | *Raising of the Daughter of Jairus* | c. 1540 | Louvre Museum, Paris, France

Page 151: Carl Bloch | *The Sermon on the Mount* | 1877 | The Museum of National History, Hillerød, Denmark

Page 153: James Tissot | *The Miracle of the Loaves and Fishes* | c. 1886–1894 | Brooklyn Museum, New York City, New York

Page 157: Giovanni Bellini | *Transfiguration of Christ* | c. 1480 | Museo di Capodimonte, Naples, Italy

Page 160: Ivan Aivazovsky | *Christ Walks on Water* | 1890 | Private Collection

Page 163: Rembrandt Harmenszoon van Rijn | *The Prodigal Son* | Hermitage Museum, Saint Petersburg, Russia

Page 167: Anthony van Dyck | *Christ Healing the Paralytic* | c. 1619 | Royal Collection, London, England

Page 170: Artist unknown | *Steel Engraving of Christ Knocking at the Door* | Date unknown

Page 173: Maurycy Gottlieb | *Christ Preaching at Capernaum* | c. 1878–1879 | National Museum in Warsaw

Page 175: Jean-Hippolyte Flandrin | *Christ's Entry into Jerusalem* | 1846 | Church of Saint-Germain-des-Prés, Paris, France

Page 177: Pieter Coecke van Aelst | *Entry of Christ into Jerusalem* | c. 1530 | Bonnefanten Museum, Maastricht, Netherlands

Page 180: Artist unknown | *Mary Magdalen Anointing Christ's Feet* | c. 1503 | National Library of Wales, Aberystwyth, Wales

Page 183: Brunswick Monogrammist | *Parable of the Great Banquet* | c. 1525 | National Museum in Warsaw, Warsaw, Poland

Page 187: Tintoretto | *Christ Washing the Disciples' Feet* | c. 1548–1549 | Museo del Prado, Madrid, Spain

Page 190: Lorenzo Lotto | *Christ the Vine and Lives of the Saints* | 1524 | Suardi Chapel, Bergamo, Italy

Page 193: Fra Angelico | *The Last Judgment* | c. 1435–1450 | Gemäldegalerie, Berlin, Germany

Page 197: Jan van Eyck | *The Ghent Altarpiece: God Almighty* (detail) | c. 1426–1427 | Saint Bavo Cathedral, Ghent, Belgium

Page 199: Raphael | *The Disputation of the Blessed Sacrament* | 1510 | Vatican Museums, Vatican City, Italy